PRAISE for THE SEVEN

"Inspiring and entertaining, The Seven R
kick-start and maintain vibrancy and resil
a small gem. I love

— **Christina Haag**, New York Times ...selling author of
Come to the Edge: A Love Story

"When two feisty, fearless females take a cross-Atlantic spree to Rome, Italy, they do more than don the adage… when in Rome! They reunite their sisterly bond on Italian shores and create a 7-step rulebook, THE SEVEN ROMAN RULES (with one bonus lesson added), to inspire, insight, and instruct us mere mortals on how to experience a more carefree, joie de vivre existence. Whether they actually channel the Roman centurion's mythical playbook, or not, may be up for discussion? But what they do come up with is an easily readable, conversational, fast-paced companion guide to letting go, feeling free, and extinguishing the limiting beliefs that have held us back in the past while gently prodding us forward with helpful tools to experience a more expansive, rich and fulfilling future. To Life! Brava bellissimas!"

— **Douglas Wickard**, Amazon bestselling author of
the *Sami Saxton* series and *FBI Detective Dan Hammer* novels

"A breezy little cruise through Rome with strappy heels and heaps of wisdom…The Petrov sisters offer practical rules for vitality, fun and wise choices as we all navigate the happy trails of womanhood. I read it in one sitting and wanted to hear more from these two, and to have the good fortune to run into them on the beach with a mojito, the perfect hat and the best novel, ever."

— **Susan Merson**, co-founder of LA Writers Bloc
and author of *Oh Good Now This*

*We dedicate this book
to our parents.*

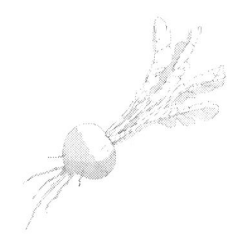

THE SEVEN ROMAN RULES

THE SEVEN ROMAN RULES

Whimsical Wisdom
From Two Sisters
On Holiday

ANNE & JANE
PETROV

A & J PUBLISHING

A & J PUBLISHING

Copyright © 2022 by Anne & Jane Petrov

All rights reserved. No part of this book may be reproduced or used in any manner without written permission of the copyright owner.

ISBN 979-8-9871699-0-2 (Paperback)
ISBN 979-8-9871699-1-9 (Ebook)
ISBN 979-8-9871699-2-6 (Hardback)
ISBN 979-8-9871699-3-3 (Audio)
ISBN 979-8-9871699-4-0 (Journal)

Book design by Lili Robins
Cover design by Angie Alaya
Illustrations by Anne Petrov
Edited by Harker Jones
Audio recording by Juan Carlos Arvelo
Interior author photo by Travis Tanner
Back cover photo by Kaela Comontofski

Visit us on the Web!
www.thesevenromanrules.com

CONTENTS

ACKNOWLEDGEMENTS — i

INTRODUCTION — iii

GLOSSARY — ix

RULE I
REJECT OLD RULES — 1

RULE II
FOLLOW THROUGH — 15

RULE III
GROW YOUR MOJO — 29

RULE IV
AGE IS IRRELEVANT — 42

RULE V
TRUST THE HEAT — 55

RULE VI
CARPE TIEMPO — 77

RULE VII
PUSH ON THROUGH — 91

BONUS RULE — 107

ACKNOWLEDGEMENTS

We are two sisters whose lives were shaped by the *joie de vivre* of our rascally Russian father and the puritanical propriety of our New England mother. We would not think these thoughts or write these words without their highly contradictory teachings. One thing they agreed on was encouraging us to have adventures. For this we are grateful.

We thank our exes for loving us and giving us food for thought. And we thank Pasquale for inviting us to his island home in the Tuscan archipelago and giving us an unexpected and much needed reprieve from our love-torn, overworked lives before traveling on to Rome. This book was conceived during that memorable trip.

We thank our numerous family members for keeping life fun. We thank Andie for literally "holding space" for us in his Hollywood home. And Elyse, who lent us her ear and provided expert feedback as we read these rules aloud to her. We thank Juan Carlos for providing us with his warm and inviting soundbooth experience. And how lucky we were to find Harker, the awesomest editor we could ever ask for. He got us.

Finally, we deeply and sincerely thank our friends who provided their feedback, wisdom, humor and testimonies during the creation of this book: Joan, Anne, Lorraine, Dara, Lainie, Sarah, Bruce, Bernadine, Kaela, Sheila, Sandra, Katya, Denise, Anne-Francoise, Vicki, Revi, Natasha, Pam and Danna.

INTRODUCTION

"All roads lead to Rome." — Anonymous

We've all heard the saying. But you don't have to go to Rome to follow these rules because Rome is a state of mind. It's about beauty and also adventure. A greater *dolce vita*. A feeling of being light, warm, open. Just plain happy. This light and happy attitude is our natural state of being. We could spend more of our time this way in our everyday lives, but how? *The Seven Roman Rules* will guide you.

We traveled to Rome after Anne's divorce and Jane's breakup. We hadn't been single at the same time for more than a few weeks ever since high school. We had dated, married, attempted motherhood and spent a few too many years "going fallow." We had not been cultivating our innate gifts or living according to our true, joyful nature. It was time to go out and smell the roses … in Rome.

This book was inspired by the magnificence and the pleasures of this unequaled city: the art, the cuisine and, yes, the men. They are hot and sexy, but they are not as self-absorbed as they could be. They know how to live and love, and they let you know it. Since we were freshly single, it seemed natural to explore the whole subject of Rome-ance. These seven rules of Rome are based on real romantic experiences and the lessons learned from them. What did we learn? And how might this knowledge enhance your *dolce vita*? This is what we share with you, Dear Reader.

After our memorable trip to Rome we left deeply satisfied after our final, sleep-free night. That morning as we rode on the airport bus, a few of these rules sprang forth from God-knows-where. We knew they were important, so Jane jotted them down on a piece of scrap paper. Additional rules revealed themselves to us in the following days. We counted: seven. How auspicious, we thought, the number seven is associated with symbolism in religion, mythology, philosophy and gambling.

We soon realized that these rules applied not just to romance, but to all kinds of relationships: with colleagues and clients, painters and plumbers, family and friends, as well as the most important relationship of all, the one you have with yourself. At the end of the day, you are in the driver's seat of your own life.

When we returned to our homes and lives, we noticed that things had subtly changed. We began to make bolder decisions and shift our priorities. Applying *The Seven Roman Rules* resulted in newfound confidence and enhanced our power to choose our own destiny. Jane finally took the plunge and moved from New York to Los Angeles to pursue film and television and go bicoastal with her production studio. Anne bought a fixer-upper in the French countryside and started learning how to use power tools.

Most of us hold back from taking risks, trying new things and living to our fullest potential. There's no room for doubt when applying *The Seven Roman Rules*. They are about taking initiative and pursuing your dreams. You decide that you're going to get up at 6 a.m. each morning and research a new career, or do yoga, or initiate two new Bumble dates. Soon you're sending out resumés, have dropped a dress size and are no longer spending Saturday night at home with a pint of Chunky Monkey.

There will be times, of course, when the joy is missing in life. Instead of a magnificent marble archway beckoning, all you see is a brick wall. That's a good time to open this book and select a rule. Meditate on it. Read through the Practice section. Then apply it and see what happens. Why not start with your love life, like we did? What do you have to lose? Tennyson rightly said, "'Tis better to have loved and lost than never to have loved at all."

Write down your thoughts and experiences. If they are mostly positive, this will encourage you to try another rule. No rule is more important than another. Also, you don't need to master one rule in order to proceed to the next. Apply them in any sequence, in a way that's right for you. But keep up the practice. Remember, "Rome wasn't built in a day."

Before you begin this epic journey, here are a few comments, disclaimers and promotional offers.

Anne initially thought this was going to be a book on how to build an empire in seven easy lessons. Jane viewed it from the get-go as a guide to help you make better choices, set the bar higher and trust your gut instincts. After due consideration, Anne agreed with Jane that there was a paucity of such handbooks on this subject and that Ben Franklin himself, the greatest American self-help guru, would probably applaud this endeavor in *Poor Richard's Almanack*.

We don't know if *The Seven Roman Rules* were channeled to us from ancient times. Or not.

They are both feminine and feminist, though we never took womyn's studies.

The seven rules can be seen as overlapping or they can be thought of as totally independent, or in scientific parlance, orthogonal in seven-dimensional space-time.

They are a *weltanschauung*. They form a philosophy or world view of their own.

In this book, a host of characters from classical Roman theatre will give their commentary. You may consult the helpful glossary at the end of this Introduction for reference.

We illustrate these rules with true stories, our own and those shared by our friends. In addition, we subpoenaed a few centurions in order to get their valuable testimonies.

What is a centurion? In the Roman legions, these were soldiers known for their valor, strength and experience, who were picked to lead a century, or one hundred soldiers. They were honored by society, exempt from public punishment and rewarded with medallions and other fancy tchotchkes.

In this book the title of centurion is bestowed upon one who has mastered the rules of Rome and can inspire and lead others in their practice. By reading these pages and trying the practice sections, you choose to take responsibility to change your life. If you find that this book doesn't serve you in any way, Jane suggests passing it along to a friend or placing it on a park bench.

We haven't been traveling much lately. But it doesn't keep us from traveling in our imagination. By writing this book, we got to revisit incredible memories. Part of living a Roman life is to create these times to look back on.

We are not therapists or life coaches. All we are is Anne and Jane, livers of life. And now, we present *The Seven Roman Rules*:

>Rule I — Reject Old Rules
>Rule II — Follow Through
>Rule III — Grow Your Mojo
>Rule IV — Age Is Irrelevant
>Rule V — Trust the Heat
>Rule VI — Carpe Tiempo
>Rule VII — Push On Through

GLOSSARY

Roman Mythology and Theatre
(The Greek names are in parentheses)

Chorus — A group of actors who comment on the main action of a play

Diana (Artemis) — The goddess of nature and the hunt

The Three Fates — Nona, Decima and Morta (Clotho, Lachesis and Atropos), weavers of a tapestry that dictates the destinies of humans

Jupiter (Zeus) — The chief Roman god, presiding over the state, its welfare and its laws; and also the sky and weather

Minerva (Athena) — The goddess of wisdom

The Three Muses — Melete, Mneme, and Aoede are the goddesses of practice, memory and song (In Greek mythology there are nine muses)

The Sibyl (Oracle) — A female seer of the future

Venus (Aphrodite) — The goddess of love and beauty

RULE I

REJECT OLD RULES

RULE I

REJECT OLD RULES

Zombies; Roman pizza; The prom; Samskara, viveka and avidya; Janet's mother's rule; Aesop's Fables; Carry and the camper; Anne and Jane in Cannes; Lauren's loss; Maria's compromise; Arianne's old and new rules

Do you recognize some of these old rules?

- Wear heels in the workplace
- Wear white only after Memorial Day
- Save the fancy china for special occasions (that rarely happen)
- Don't eat dessert before finishing your dinner
- The guy should make the first move

We've all been there, at least the Gen X-ers and Boomers among us. We were taught by our parents and other elders how to behave and follow the rules of society. This teaching was reinforced in schools, by Miss Manners, women's magazines and old television shows. How much of this is plain old common sense and how much of it is based on *zombie conformity?* Zombies don't think for themselves.

Jane inquires, "Have you noticed how many zombie movies are out there these days? Not to mention zombie television shows, toys, books, apparel and commercials. There's even a zombie Christmas movie musical! What's up with that? Has anybody bothered to ask this question?" Anne replies, "It's the *zeitgeist.*" Jane asks, "The what-geist?" They google it: "*Zeitgeist* is the defining spirit or mood of a particular period of history as shown by the ideas and beliefs of the time." Jane affirms, "A-ha, that's why so many people relate to zombies."

Who has ever felt like they were caught between the living and the dead, with no light at the end of the tunnel, in a life situation that has gone way past the sell-by date? Who *hasn't?* Well, Dear Reader, this stuff is par for the course for zombies but not for centurions. Is this relevant to following this Roman Rule? Abso-f-ing-lutely! Doing what everybody else does because you're "supposed to" is zombie. It is simply not Roman.

Anne drives this point home with pizza. She says, "Roman pizza breaks the old rules and does it with pizzazz. They seem enormous, but the crust is impossibly thin and crisp, and it's wonderfully flavored with only the merest smidge of succulent tomato sauce. As for the toppings, there are almost none: an olive here, a basil leaf there, but each mouthful is a testament to the glory of Rome."

If you do a deep inquiry, really look at a stagnant situation, you may find that you've unconsciously been following an old rule that no longer applies. Therefore, we have to question. We have to check in, not check out. We have to exercise the ability to Reject Old Rules!

To illustrate, let's examine a period in life when a whopping number of old rules are forged: high school. Several strong and sometimes conflicting influences are at work—you want to fit in with your friends, you want your parents' approval and you are just beginning to know yourself.

Consider this pivotal event: the prom. You're waiting to be asked by a boy you really like, but another boy asks you first. You don't say yes, because you hardly know him. You go home and tell your mother and she says something that sounds very strange: You have to accept the invitation. Why? Because he asked you first and it will put a feather in his cap. It takes a while for her perplexing response to sink in. You imagine the boy wearing a Robin Hood cap. It doesn't make sense. But at age sixteen, you abide by her rule and accept the invitation. That's an old rule.

On said prom night, said boy who never spoke to you before the said invitation, shows up in a pale blue tux with bad skin and puffy hair. No chemistry here, folks. Even though you want to run screaming into the night, once you get to the dance you try to act like you are having a good time. Another old rule. After the prom, he walks you to your front door. You are obliged to kiss him good night. Oh, yes, a big old-fashioned rule. He paid for the night, after all. And that's a rule, too.

This example illustrates several old rules. Did they serve you in any way, shape or form? Hell, no! What happened to your own good judgment? Why not politely turn down the first invitation and wait for one from somebody you like, and really want to kiss, or just go with a friend?

Sorry to be ominous, but this stuff is habit-forming and habits make up your character and that can change your destiny. In yoga, these habits are called *samskaras*. They stay embedded in the memory banks for a good long time, Dear Reader. The above example was from high school where many patterns get established, and unless something lucky happens or you

Reject Old Rules, you may never find your soul mate. Yogis talk about another concept, called *viveka*, which is looking at a situation with discernment. Another concept, called *avidya,* is like a veil that gets flung over knowledge, making you ignorant for a while. Basically, more *viveka* and less *avidya* is the way to go. As is going with your gut. Why be inauthentic? Why learn to pretend? Create good *samskaras.* Reject Old Rules.

Back to high school; were you taught to let the guy call you? Anne never initiated a phone call to the guy she was attracted to because of the rule: The guy should call the girl. Why? And just because a guy calls, does that mean we have to accept? Jane observes, "I think we were taught to acquiesce rather than invite or refuse. And nobody told us why." The question of who should initiate a date, the man or the woman, seems to be generational. Younger women may sally forth; older women may hold out.

The sisters sought expert testimony on this important subject from their wise friend Janet, a distinguished former U.S. ambassador with the body of a Bond girl. Janet's voice drops an octave, "My mother had only one rule: Never call a man." She continues, her green-eyed gaze unwavering, "If you do call, then you're chasing him. You're not a challenge and he's off to the next woman. Things may have changed a bit, but no matter what, don't call."

Dear Reader, this weighty counsel comes from a laurel-wreathed centurion of the highest rank, one who proposed a pithier title for this chapter, "Fuck Old Rules," and yet has never broken her mother's rule. We may call this the paradox of the paradigm. Jane ponders this one and says, "It's just like a Rubik's Cube. People will be trying to figure out what that means for decades."

How many of us accept old rules that bind us to endless responsibilities at the expense of spontaneity and fun? We have one of Aesop's fables to remind us about this, *The Ant and the Grasshopper*. The ant works nonstop and gets through the winter in his tunnels while the grasshopper plays his music all summer long and freezes in the fall. Reject Old Rules is not about bucking all obligations, but rather taking time to play that violin, relax and chill out. Our schedules get so packed that we stop peppering in the fun of life. It may feel scary to reject that impulse to go, go, go. But we could all scale back a little: accept a less demanding job, own a smaller house, drive a used car, "check in" more with loved ones and with ourselves. Rejecting old rules may mean lying on the couch and getting some rest.

Our younger sister, Carry, a busy financial adviser, bought an amazing camper for herself and her twelve-year-old son to enjoy the great outdoors. She got a new SUV to pull it around, learned how to back it up and made plans to redo the driveway to park it by the house. But she had a problem. "I have no idea when I'll be able to take it on a vacation," she sighed. Anne chimed in helpfully, "Your responsibilities include having as much fun as you can with your boy and enjoying his youth." Jane barked, "Your boss loves you. You run the fuckin' show. You think he's gonna toss you to the curb? Tell him you're taking two weeks off. Your son will be sixteen before you know it!" Carry considered the old rule, i.e. work overtime and skimp on vacation. Then she thought about rejecting it: "Maybe I could take a week off and work remotely from the camper in a state park. Then Walter can play video games and go fishing. And I can watch my news and Netflix!" Jane commended her on this Roman compromise, "That's the spirit, *teleglamp!*"

What about an old rule that says something like "You can't have fun until you finish some soul-crushing drudgery or other bullshit"? Why not? We're all trying to become earnest centurions here. We're not talking about flaking out on family, work or community responsibilities. But what about having fun intentionally as a goal, rather than as a reward?

A few years back, Anne and Jane were talking on the phone about meeting up in Cannes for the film festival. Jane had wanted to go for years but she was hesitating because she didn't have a film project to pitch. Anne said she had to put up drywall. Jane grumbled, "The old rule is we don't deserve to go have fun. Of course we should be responsible; I need to find a backer and you need to do renovation work on your property in France. But why do you need to put up drywall during the few precious days of Cannes?" Anne and Jane *paused*. They could almost hear each other breathe. Neither had ever been to Cannes. They could either spend the next fifteen years talking about how they should have gone *or* invoke this Roman Rule and balance work with fun. So here is a Roman pop quiz.

Did Anne:

1. Buy a ticket there and then?
2. Wait and pay double?
3. Stay home and do drywall?
4. Do none of the above (i.e. be a loser because indecision is un-Roman)?

Here is what happened. Jane talked to her friend Dave who said, "Hell, if you go to Cannes you can pitch my film and I'll pay half of your expenses!" So she ended up going to Cannes and Anne went, too, and they had the time of their lives. And ... Jane closed a deal for a film.

How does the puritan work ethic and Aesop's fable of *The Ant and the Grasshopper* affect your love life?

The old rule that puts responsibility at the top of everyone's to-do list can be a killer in your relationships. How many of us have been in a relationship where "us" always comes last? Anything else comes first: laundry, the in-laws, the lawn, football season. How many married couples wait until the kids are in school, or out of school, or until retirement to finally have "us" time?

Anne's old friend Lauren from ninth grade is a computer scientist with pure gray eyes. She had been married for twenty-four years, had a beautiful home and excellent kids, and took care of her parents who lived in the extension off her garage. Just after her youngest son's high school graduation, her husband, out of nowhere, told her he was leaving and handed her separation papers. A few weeks later, Anne visited Lauren who said, "We were just at the point where there would be time for us. Our son finally got his driver's license so there's no more driving him everywhere."

The two friends sat on the living room couch, creamy White Russians in one hand, tragic masks in the other. Lauren raised her mask and said, "It was more than the loss of the marriage. It was the loss of my family, my husband, my planned future. I knew none of it would ever be what it was again. Poof! It was all gone." Anne raised her mask in silent sympathy and said, "Sometimes a centurion must navigate the seas that seem to swallow her up."

When things don't work out, all we can do is learn and move on. Last we looked, there are no associate degrees for building love partnerships. Dear Reader, we are navigating with you.

The noble centurion Arianne is a vivacious eighty-one-year-old from San Francisco who retired to Nice, on the French Riviera. Anne obtained her testimony, which spanned the women's lib era. Here's what she said, "I was brought up in the age where you couldn't just get married to a steelworker, settle down and be a housewife. You were supposed to get a degree and make something of your life. That was one half of it. But the other half was that you were supposed to fall in love and get married. That was the culture of the times. In psychology textbooks they were still teaching that people were only 'successful' if they were capable of having an intimate relationship. So I adopted the idea that you had to get married, have kids, live in the suburbs and be successful or there was something wrong with you. I can hardly believe how much crap I actually bought into hook, line and sinker. And I was progressive and way ahead of my time."

Anne asks, "How did things pan out with those rules?" Arianne laughs, "I got a PhD from Stanford and I had three disastrous marriages. My biggest secret and the beginning of my true happiness was the day that I said, 'This is over for me. I'm giving up those expectations. I am going to be my own best friend. If I bring somebody into my life, he has to live down the hall.' It was a psychological transformation for me. It was such a relief, a huge burden that wasn't there anymore."

A different kind of rule-breaking is illustrated by Maria, a lovely and patient former administrative assistant. She was tired of the struggle. She had been single since college. All she wanted was to get married, have a balanced checkbook and be able to buy steak. She married a decent man with plenty in the bank, had two beautiful children and hadn't had sex in years. She confided in Jane, her friend since seventh grade, "I'm happy to be in this relationship because this is what I want for my life. It's not about giving in, it's my choice." Maria rejected the rule that says you must have passion in your marriage à la 1950s Hollywood movies. Jane admired Maria's pretty house and garden. She understood her friend's compromise and noticed the wreath of laurel that ringed her blonde curls.

The good news is "All roads lead to Rome." So if your thing is security, backyard barbeques and building your 401(k), then so be it. You have made a choice that suits you. What may seem like a ho-hum life to one centurion is bliss to another.

With this inspiration, we call on you, Dear Reader, to exercise your own wisdom in knowing which old rules to just throw out.

PRACTICE

Let's reframe the list of common old rules in a Roman light:

- Wearing heels in the workplace becomes ... **put on sexy, flat-soled, thigh-high boots.**
- Wearing white only after Memorial Day becomes ... **drape yourself in a white pashmina scarf at Christmas.**
- Saving the fancy china for special occasions becomes ... **take your boring stoneware to the Salvation Army and fill your kitchen cabinets with the good stuff.**
- No dessert before finishing your dinner becomes ... **order an appetizer and follow it with your favorite, decadent dessert.**

Try to reframe a few old rules. Who says you have to conform to this? Who says you have to do that? When it comes right down to it: You do. You are the only one in the driver's seat.

One ancient yogic practice involves replacing a negative thought with the positive version of the same thought. For example, "I am an uninteresting zombie" becomes "I have a sparkling personality." How can we apply this technique to practicing Reject Old Rules with our partner? Instead of saying "It's selfish to go to Cabo with my husband" say "The kids would love it if they were in charge at home with Grandma." Instead of saying "I'm greedy if I spend a weekend with my girlfriends at the beach" say "Perhaps my husband would like to go fly-fishing with the guys." Instead of saying, "I don't know if he's ready to have kids" ask him, "Would you like to make a baby with me?"

As for dating or finding a life partner, a particular category where old rules run deep, the Roman approach is to let the man know you are interested. Practice this in any way you like. It could be subtle, like a wink, a smile or a touch on a shoulder. Or it could be really bold, like picking him up from the airport wearing nothing but a trench coat.

Be creative, oh, centurions!

RULE II

FOLLOW THROUGH

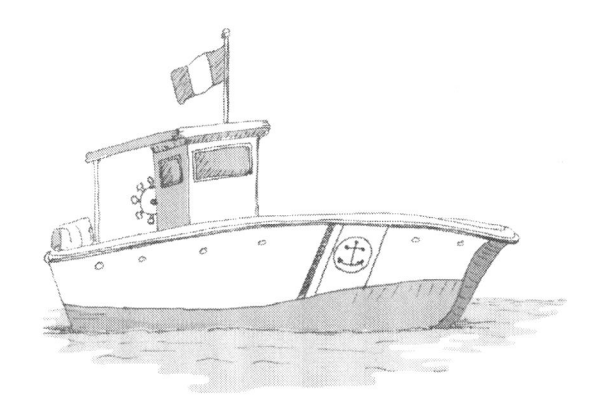

RULE II

FOLLOW THROUGH

Alice's to-do list; Roadblocks to action; The Captain and the Police Chief; Jane's production deal; Chloe's light bulb; Linda goes to Kathmandu; Never say "What if?"

Follow Through is Jane's signature rule. It's about completion. It's about who-does-what-by-when. It's about accountability with yourself, making sure you've done your due diligence by taking action and, most importantly, making certain the communication circle is complete.

By following through on communication there will be fewer problems in your personal and work relationships. It quiets your questioning. You don't have to ask yourself: Did he understand the urgency of my last email? Does she need a follow-up call? Folks, just by following through, you won't miss out on stuff. You'll send a lot fewer "Happy Belated" missives.

You can live with yourself. This frees up your energy, mental space and focus for important things instead of stupid shit.

An unfocused mind is not light. You carry around a lot of mental burden when the same things pop up on your to-do list every day. Jane chats with her friend Alice, a gorgeous and gifted thespian, who describes her battles with to-do list overwhelm, "I can't get through it all. So, I don't do any of it. Do we ever finish what's on our list?" Jane shares her brother-in-law's technique, "Phil only puts two or three things on his list each day, that way he finishes them." Alice exclaims, "I cleaned the bathroom! But that wasn't on my list." Jane concedes, "Well, then, put it on your list, then cross it off."

Alice loved shelter in place during the pandemic; nobody could go anywhere. She checked out of social media and resisted the impulse to stay in touch with everybody, every day. For the first time in her life, she felt like she wasn't playing catch-up. She didn't need to-do lists. She could finally take a breath.

Jane ruminates, "I bet the things on our to-do lists will still be hanging around when we meet our maker." Anne mulls this over, "In yoga, tamas is when you feel so inert that you just let stuff slide. You may care but you don't have the mental or physical energy to do anything about it." Jane comments, "Poor eating habits can also be a factor, but that's a whole separate book!" People who habitually don't follow through will resist this rule and may skip forward. The rest of you know this rule means you'll have to put your Big Girl Pants on. Please, read on.

A person who follows through is a leader. Centurions *always* circle back; they try to communicate one more time. Follow Through is about integrity, the power of one's word. This rule always made sense to Jane, whether she was producing a film, coaching actors or cleaning toilets.

She is adamant, saying, "If I say I'm going to do something, I do it. If I don't, I let myself down and will feel guilty." Anne inquires, "Do you want to come clean on anything?" Jane confesses, "I missed a colleague's show after I RSVP'd on her Facebook invite that I would go." Anne nudges, "How would you follow your signature rule here?" Jane hedges, "I could come up with a bunch of lame excuses, but the bottom line is, I need to follow through with a call and apologize. It's already been a week." Sometimes that week can turn into months, folks, and then you really feel lame.

Here are some roadblocks that keep us from owning our actions and following through:

- Laziness — You intentionally put things off. *Perhaps you smoke too much weed?*
- Procrastination — You don't enjoy doing something so you do something else. *That's Anne's specialty.*
- Fatigue — You're not getting to the gym, you're not eating well, you party too much. *And ... perhaps you smoke too much weed?*
- Non-Commitment — You're practicing the Hollywood shuffle with people: "Let's do lunch sometime!" "Absolutely!" *Then two years go by.*

A big reason we don't practice this rule is Fear and its best friend, Doubt. Jane gives an example that she's been dealing with in her own business: "I've been trying to get a potential client to sign a new video production deal. Weeks have gone by and she still hasn't responded to my proposal."

Anne inquires, "What do you think is going on?" Jane thinks out loud, "Maybe I'm afraid she doesn't want to work with me, or maybe she found someplace cheaper." Anne remarks, "Most of us have trouble with doubt and imagined fears. But in most cases people are not avoiding you intentionally, they're just caught up in their own lives."

Jane says, "Right. I'm just filling up space in my head wondering, 'Is there something that she doesn't like about me? Is that why she's avoiding me?'" Anne suggests, "So why not take the lead?"

Jane agrees, "Yeah. What's keeping me from calling and asking her directly, 'Hey, Julie, I know you wanted to shoot this winter. Let me know if this is in the cards for you in January.'?" A pause ensues. Now what? Anne and Jane exchange glances and say in unison, "Call her now!"

You see, Dear Reader, we are with you. We are out there, following through to the best of our abilities. Even the smallest action forward is bold and brave.

Before we go further, let's pause for *Pause*, a vital tool for implementing *The Seven Roman Rules*. When you have applied a rule diligently to a situation and you are blocked, we recommend that you pause at that point. Stop all action.

The great orators of ancient Rome knew about *Pause*. Remember these famous words: "Friends, Romans, Countrymen, lend me your ears." People had more patience back then to listen to orators. They had less to do. They didn't have to hurry home to Hulu. Actors who pause bring power to their scenes. Inspirational speakers choose when to pause so that the listener can absorb information. They know not to data dump. *Pause* is not Menopause. It is not Men. It is not No. In music, it is the rest after the measure. In writing, it's the ellipsis at the edge of a sentence. Stillness. Breath. Maybe three breaths.

Dear Reader, we don't want you to be impulsive or reckless when applying the Roman Rules. The rules are about action. *Pause* is the space between actions. It's letting the thoughts settle so that the answers come. It is good to *pause*.

You may want to know what came of Jane's exchange with her potential client. Did she book the shoot? "Hell, no!" Jane replied. "Julie acted interested, but she kept kicking the can down the road. It was the classic Hollywood shuffle. Finally, I drilled down to get an answer and she said she didn't have the money. It was that simple. I didn't have to keep barking up her tree. I could check that off my list. Free up some brain space."

What about practicing this rule in a new relationship? To illustrate, Anne and Jane fondly recollect their holiday with Anne's friend Pasquale on an island paradise off the Tuscan coast. Each day the sisters would stroll down to the lovely beach to swim. In the evening they'd wander into the fishing village to buy sweet, creamy gelato, then head to their favorite terrace bar to mingle with the locals. At night the young chief of police would walk Jane home, and they'd kiss on the terrace. He always wanted more. The coast guard captain, a Sicilian, would walk with Anne. He expressed his desire to get married and have a baby with her. Things move fast in Italy.

Jane inquires, "The Captain was a lot younger than you, right?" Anne replies, "Well, yes, but I thought he was older. He was attractively balding, remember?"

Jane recalls that Anne and the Captain had problems with their communication from the start: "He'd invite you to meet up but then leave you hanging about where and when." Anne admits, "Well, there was that time we met at his boat. I think he wanted me to see him in uniform." She sighs, recollecting the little Coast Guard skiff on the turquoise water and the Captain dressed in white from shoes to smile. Jane pursues, "You were ready to go to Sicily and start a life as an Italian wife! What happened? Now I remember. There was that moment on the island when I told you to call him and you said, 'No!' What kept you from following through?" There is no response from Anne. Jane continues, "I think you got stuck on an old rule, 'The guy has to call the girl.'" Still no response from Anne. Jane concludes resoundingly, "You should have rejected that!"

Black clouds suddenly gather above. Thunder rumbles and a bolt of lightning zigzags across the sky, writing the portent: *Remember Janet's Mother's Rule from Chapter One: Never Call a Man!* The Roman Gods and Goddesses observe the sisters in their struggle with this rule. Jane shouts to the heavens: "You *must* make the effort. *You* must Follow Through."

The sun gently re-emerges. Anne says quietly, "I admit, I was waiting for his call for a couple of days. That was in pre-Roman times. Procrastination, I have that, too." Jane says, "Fear. Fear of rejection. Don't we all have that?" The sisters nod in agreement. The challenges of the practice are great indeed. Jane suggests, "If a guy you like has asked you out but hasn't provided the details, call him. Leave a message. Step up to the plate. *You* can ask *him*, 'How about a gelato?'" Anne agrees, "Follow Through, make the call, then the ball is in *his* court." "Exactly," Jane concludes. "Then you can live with yourself. Then you don't have to ask yourself on the flight home, should I have called him back?"

How did their week on the sun-kissed island end, you may ask? Anne followed through and called the Captain. He invited Jane's police chief, and the two couples met on a quiet beach surrounded by gently sloping vineyards. Anne wore her new, tamale-red, cleavage-spilling one-piece. Jane wore her sky-blue bikini. They all shared a bottle of Chianti, and then the couples wandered off in different directions. The men spread towels on the hot sand. They applied sunscreen to the women's shoulders. Anne learned that her Captain had to suddenly go back to Sicily. Jane learned that her Chief was married. Like we said before, things move fast in Italy. Anne says, "I was glad we followed through. That way, we learned the truth." Jane agrees, "Yeah. We got played. But we sure had fun playing."

The Roman Chorus chimes in: "The sisters were heading to Rome the next day. They knew there were still plenty of fish in the sea."

The above example illustrates a corollary to this Roman Rule, first uttered by Lauren, the centurion of the pure gray eyes. "Never say *what if*," spake Lauren. "Regardless of what happens in life, if you Follow Through, you don't have to spend years wondering, 'What if I had …?'"

Follow Through is taking something to completion to the best of your knowledge and abilities. We can only begin to describe all of the amazing benefits of practicing this rule. Here are a few of them: peace, lightness, a clean house, a clear conscience and, perhaps, an island romance.

Practicing this rule can be altruistic, a good deed for the day, making another person feel better. You can strive to practice it in unpleasant situations, like after a misunderstanding with a client. You can practice it when you get your feelings hurt by a friend or lover. You can reach out to them to clear the air. You are doing a positive thing and that will circle back to you.

A focused mind is a key ingredient in practicing this rule. Linda, a stunning yoga and Pilates instructor, life coach and dog owner, kept herself constantly busy with three jobs. She would develop professional contacts, start creative projects, then get distracted and rarely Follow Through. Linda didn't think she had enough hours in the day to finish anything. One day she decided to quit her jobs and fly all the way from Los Angeles to Kathmandu where she hoped to learn about life from wise yogis in the Himalayas. In temples and ashrams Linda learned that her conscious choices mattered. She discovered that constantly busying herself stunted her mental focus and thus her ability to Follow Through. So she decided to go to India and learn meditation. There she began to focus her mind and finally realized that all she needed was a regular routine and rest.

Linda had to go all the way to Nepal and India to master this rule. Perhaps you, too, can quit your job and go to India. It's a trend. But you can save a lot of time and money by practicing this rule at home, especially with the convenience of Zoom and Google Hangouts.

Follow Through requires emotional admin work. You have to take the time to explain to another person what you want *and*, just as importantly, you have to listen to what *they* want. It is not "Can't you just 'get me' and roll with it?" The answer is, "No." Sometimes you have to engage deeply with other people. Take responsibility. Follow Through means taking a risk and being vulnerable. You may fear getting hurt, but we assure you that nine times out of ten, you will end up with a positive outcome, even if it's *just* peace of mind, which is extremely valuable these days.

This rule is a must for any successful relationship. A common pitfall with this rule is that you may think you can put conditions on your significant other and the way they Follow Through.

Chloe is an elegant cougar and her youthful boyfriend, Max, loves and adores her. One day Chloe called Jane in a tiff because her beau wasn't phoning her when he said he would. He was on a trip, visiting family. As a business leader, skilled at "Who does what by when," Chloe put conditions on how her boyfriend practiced Follow Through with her. But that can bite you in the butt when you apply it to your lover. Jane counseled,

"Give Max a break. He's on holiday and he's having family time. He's not your account executive."

You have to have patience, trust and flexibility to be open to your partner's way of responding. Chloe, fortunately, has an uncommonly high IQ. The light bulb went on when she talked to Jane. She realized that her love relationship was different from a business relationship, and that was a wonderful thing. Now she gives Max the space to Follow Through in his own way.

PRACTICE

As you read these words, put this book down. Go get a pen and write three things you have to Follow Through on, and do those things this week. Deal? When they're done, check them off your list. You will feel so much better and be ready for three more items.

Mastering this rule, like any of the seven rules, is a noble achievement. But practicing it is the main goal. Once you begin to enjoy the results you'll feel encouraged to keep on practicing at your own pace. It's not a race.

Do you think your Maker's up there saying, "You got behind on this!"? Heck, no! What matters is taking action. Are you not following through because you are prideful? Are you feeling wronged? Here is an important reminder: When you practice this rule, don't let your pride get in the way. If there is miscommunication, be kind and speak with sincerity. Rather than asking, "WTF? Don't you get it?" you could say, "Forgive me if I'm not being clear. Let me try to say this differently."

Maybe you've had a disagreement with a colleague or secretary. Maybe you've made a pledge to send a real letter to your niece on a special occasion. Maybe you forgot to call your best friend on her birthday. Jane reminds us, "The humble pie thing is where it's at."

So call, write, Zoom. Remember the old telephone ad jingle, "Reach out and touch someone." And text, if you must, as a last resort.

Come on, there are no excuses. Follow Through.

RULE III

GROW YOUR MOJO

RULE III

GROW YOUR MOJO

Cranky Jane; What is mojo?; Jane does karaoke; Ann Cole's song; Yogi ojas; Dad's clackers; Arianne's tango; Stacy and the fun bus; Sexiness; High school grooming

Jane is cranky. She complains, "I'm overworked, treading water and I don't give a rat's ass about my health. This year is already in the shitter. Eh, I guess there's always next year." Anne retorts, "It's only July and you're already writing off the whole doggone year?" Jane is determined to stay cranky, saying, "I dealt with five clients, negotiated a film contract and got through my boring day job. I push myself every day to make the bucks to pay the bills, and then I go to bed."

Sound familiar? Sure, Jane is making ends meet, she's even overachieving, but clearly she's not enjoying the journey. She's outta gas. She's in a funk. Her inner child has been put on ice. Yeah, she gets it, it's self-sabotage. What is the Roman explanation for her state of being? Jane's mojo ain't working.

"What is mojo?" Jane asks. Anne has known about mojo for quite some time but she doesn't think it's a real word in the dictionary. They google it: "A quality that attracts people to you and makes you successful and full of energy ... *Mojo* (African-American culture) may refer to a magical charm bag used in voodoo ... Libido is sometimes referred to in slang as *mojo*." So mojo is confidence, charisma, magnetism.

Jane continues her mojo-less moping: "I've had a $250 Victoria's Secret gift card from my boyfriend burning a hole in my wallet since Christmas. Why bother with sexy lingerie when we got the dog in the bed?" Anne probes, "You must have done at least one fun thing this year. What about that karaoke night?" Jane's eyes sparkle and a reluctant smile appears. "Oh, yeah, when I decided to dress up and go out with my friends Sergio and Fred." Anne eggs her on, saying, "What did you wear?" Jane recollects, "I put on a little black dress and my high boots with the flat heels, and with those boots I felt great. I went on stage and sang the Chicks and everybody loved it." That experience was spontaneous, reaffirming and a 10 on the mojo-meter. It reignited Jane's *joie de vivre*. She reminisces for a moment then says, "I may just go to Victoria's Secret and spend that gift card. Hah!" Anne gives her a high five.

This Roman Rule says: *Get your mojo working!* Just like the song written by Preston "Red" Foster and first recorded in 1956 by sassy Ann Cole, the mother of mojo, and popularized by blues legend Muddy Waters. Anne insists that this song is a must-hear for centurions. She herself sings it when she's strollin' on the boardwalk in the Riviera: "I got my mojo workin' ..."

Yogis believe that our bodies contain tiny amounts of a subtle substance called *ojas*, which is derived from pure food, fresh air and water. It is the essence of our vitality, and if a yogi stores up her *ojas* rather than frittering it away, she can survive winters in the Himalayas and other challenges. Anne says, "*Ojas* and mojo … the words sound similar, right?" Jane agrees, "Where else can you get such a wide range of useful information but in *The Seven Roman Rules?*"

Thinking of vitality, Anne remembers that their father used to tell his teenage offspring, "Don't shuffle your feet!" And he set the example. She recalls, "He'd have the shoe repairman nail taps on his shoes to remind him to pick up his step. Then he'd stride down K Street in Washington, D.C. with his new *clackers* on." Jane smiles and says, "He wanted to have a youthful step. He had mojo." Anne adds, "And shuffling reminded him of prisoners he knew when he was in the gulag." Jane asks, "Really? I didn't know that. I mean, I knew he clacked, but I didn't know there was a whole story behind it. That's funny. It's like *Hints from Heloise,* Russian gulag-style."

Instead of keeping their mojo up, people will find excuses for letting it remain low, such as: "I'm always working," "I've been married for years" or "I'm in menopause." We get numb and then the zombie factor creeps in. We stop trying as our mojo keeps sinking. We may even resort to, "Maybe I need to go have an affair." Dear Reader, that probably isn't necessary.

Anne and Jane remember the predicament of their friend Stacy, a neighbor from their D.C. days. She had been stuck at home in the suburbs for most of the year. She badly needed a break from the pizza truck business that her husband, Jim, was running from their garage, complete with sweaty twelve-hour shifts and zero days off. Stacy's mojo was no mo'. Jane says, "She needed a getaway weekend but she couldn't convince Jim."

Anne comments on these dire situations we get ourselves into, saying, "Often we run ourselves ragged, ignoring our physical and emotional selves, and hope that our partner will notice that we need a break." Jane observes, "I hate to break it to you, but Jim was as happy as a pig in shit. Sounded like he was having a love affair with his pizza business instead of his wife." Anne chimes in, "Sure, Jim's focus was on the business, but Stacy had to focus on herself. Sometimes we have to step off the gas and practice self-care, otherwise we end up becoming a shadow of ourselves. This is a first step toward getting our mojo back." Jane takes in this truth, then is reminded of their younger sister's knack for self-care and getaways: "Remember how Carry was heading down to the Keys on a fun bus with singles, couples and their drinking-age kids? I told Stacy to get on that bus with her." Anne's eyes light up and she says, "That trip was a great idea. It got Stacy's mojo working."

Everybody must find their own way to grow their mojo. In her famous song, Ann Cole uses magic charms to get her mojo working.

The three Muses spell it out:

"Some folks have their voodoo and their rabbit's foot," whispers Melete.

"Others have their *ojas* and their clackers," chuckles Mneme.

"Some folks are lucky and some folks ain't, but everyone can grow their mojo," counsels Aoide.

Grow Your Mojo is the essence of *The Seven Roman Rules*, yet it is probably the hardest rule to grasp. The mysteries of mojo run deep and there are myriad sources of confusion. You're seeking answers, asking, "Do I have to get a rabbit's foot?" Unfortunately, our blues legends didn't leave us any more clues. Anne admits, "This practice is difficult." Jane agrees, "I think I'm better at some of the other Roman Rules."

The sisters decide to seek expert testimony from the valiant centurion Arianne, who is currently living in Nice, as you may recall. She spells out her source of mojo saying, "The tango is my love. I used to go three or four times a week. It's very sexual and sensual. And every time I get a good dance partner, it's like I'm falling in love. In the past, I would get that energy and then I'd get depressed, because I thought I couldn't have it without, you know, dating him and settling down. But now I just enjoy that energy without the expectation. It's so liberating, it's wonderful. Such an intimate kind of connection."

The three Muses nod in unison and give each other a high five.

Dear Reader, can you guess what happened when Stacy went to Key West and enjoyed the camaraderie of the fun-bus gang? She returned tanned and refreshed. She was happy and looked sexy. To welcome Stacy home, Jim prepared a special wine-and-cheese plate and promised they'd take a week off together the next time. Anne observes, "If she hadn't gone when she did, she probably would have lost her mojo completely." Jane adds, "Jim got the memo on how to make Stacy happy."

Let's contemplate these ancient chariot bumper stickers:

I Rock Thigh-High Boots

Clackers Beat Shuffling

Nobody Cares How Hard You Work All Week

Give Him The Memo With A Bull Horn

Jane wants to rap on a subject that is intimately connected with mojo: sexiness. She wonders, "Why is the subject of sexiness not really discussed? Do you ever hear your girlfriends talk about it? I don't." She describes a lingerie fashion show she recently watched on television. "I was enthralled. Those young women were so gorgeous, slender, with long torsos and no belly fat at all. So flirty and full of mojo. When a reporter asked about the sexiness they displayed, one of the models said, 'It's just for us, we enjoy it.' That was interesting to me. They weren't doing it to seduce anybody; they were just having fun and sassing around for themselves."

Anne has a small epiphany, "Back when we were in high school, we did our hair and makeup, but it wasn't necessarily for the boys or for being accepted. It just felt better that way."

Grooming is part of growing your mojo. Cleansing and decorating the body is a quality of all human cultures. Jane reminisces, "I admired the girls who came to school well-coiffed and in fashion, with impressive bazooms. You and I would do the quick version of what the other girls did to stand out." Anne agrees, "We didn't have time for such maintenance. I relied on my skills as the class clown." Jane says, "Anne, you had mojo."

If you're feeling good, like your true self, then your mojo is bound to be working, like Arianne's is, at the age of eighty-one. Mojo is self-confidence. It is a quality behind sexiness. You don't need to be perfect to have mojo but you do need to have fun.

Anne and Jane have certainly learned things together. Remember how Jane was cranky at the beginning of this chapter? Well, soon afterward she discovered she had breast cancer. Months of treatment woke her up to the need to pay attention to her health, create a positive mindset and release stress. And, just so you know, she's cancer free, enjoying *joie de vivre* and her mojo is working, most of the time.

Let's not let this slide, folks, let's be mojo coaches for each other. Grow Your Mojo and keep it working. That's the rule. So, Dear Reader, pour some wine (or coconut water), put on something you think is sexy, get up now and dance to Ann Cole's version of "Got My Mojo Working."

PRACTICE

What does a Roman centurion do when her mojo-meter is on *zero*? We admit that we can't all go to the Florida Keys and party at the drop of a hat. First, recognize when your mojo is low; figure it out for yourself or ask a close friend. *Pause*. Then you can communicate better. This is a huge responsibility. In such instances, if your lover wants to argue, you can say, "I'm not myself right now, Honey. Can we talk when I get back from walking the dog?" Or if your business partner is pressuring you and you're not on your game, say, "Can we talk later when I've reviewed the financials?"

Next, take restorative steps to remedy the situation and Grow Your Mojo. Okay, you don't have to go out and sing karaoke in front of people you don't know, but you can get a new haircut, or get a massage. Anne says, "When I'm rested and relaxed, my mojo-meter goes up." She speaks for many of us. You may need more self-care. Stay in on the weekend, lie on the couch for a few hours or get yourself back into the yoga studio. If you're single, update your old online dating profile and add the hottest new photos of yourself.

Then, go deeper into the practice of this rule. It could be about sensations, burning incense or going out and ordering seafood. "Seafood is sexy food," says Jane. "I don't know why. Maybe because it's expensive." The practice is also about developing a sense of play. Jane recalls a YouTube video of old ladies in a retirement home being served their holiday meal by male dancers in little red G-strings. She says, "That's going to be you and me in retirement."

Mojo can be grown in so many ways! A sense of adventure and traveling to new places builds mojo. One such place is Rome. Imagine a graceful square, buildings stuccoed in shades of ocher and pastel. You listen to accordion music and the lyrical language spoken around you. As you sip a delicious cappuccino you consider all of the possibilities that the day might present. Everywhere you look there are attractive, swarthy Italian men on the streets and in the cafés. You cannot possibly engage with all of them but you may savor their presence, like statues of Michelangelo coming to life, smiling and riding Vespas.

"They don't have to do much," Jane notes. "So true," Anne concurs.

In Rome, Anne and Jane were ready to experience passion if the opportunity presented itself. Meanwhile, they trained. They bought shoes that were so hot they had to show their IDs at the time of purchase. They dined in restaurants where the food was simple, yet succulently seductive, so that romance was kindled between fork and mouth. And taking in a monument or neighborhood of unearthly beauty during the day prepared them for the nights.

How can you get into a Roman state of mind without the plane ticket? "Share a glass of wine, preferably Chianti, with your sweetheart. Then watch a romantic black and white movie," Anne suggests. Jane adds, "Drive to Santa Monica and have drinks at the Hotel Casa del Mar. Do a night out. Go dancing." Anne remarks, "You know how to create occasions." Jane agrees, "I like to light candles when people come over for dinner. We never lit candles growing up, except for Christmas or birthdays. They add a special quality." Anne sighs, *"Gemütlichkeit."* Jane says, "What? I didn't sneeze." Anne explains, "It's that special ambience, like mojo in your home."

Anne and Jane *pause*. Then Jane says, "There's really no substitute for Rome, quite honestly. I would go every year if I could. People tell me, 'You can't go to Rome, it costs too much.' Or they say, 'I can't believe that for someone who's got no money you're always going to Europe.' Well, what I say to that is, I deprive myself of other things. I don't do clothes. My car is fifteen years old. I've replaced everything twice. So guess what? I'm going to Rome as soon as I can."

RULE IV

AGE IS IRRELEVANT

RULE IV

AGE IS IRRELEVANT

A young fuddy-duddy; Yoga and prana; Exercise!; Learning at any age; Skipping in Washington, D.C.; Climb a tree; Rock climb naked; Age and clothes; Piazza Navona; Jane and Marco; Own the lines; Arianne's tango; Sarah's puzzle; Sex when you're older; Janet's caveat

When Anne and Jane's mother was in her final years she'd give this ironic advice: "Don't grow old." How many times have you heard the following expression, "Youth is wasted on the young"? Anne says, "*Balderdash*!" Jane retorts, "What? I have no idea what that word means." Anne explains, "It means nonsense. You can grow old with spirit and style, just like you can be a young fuddy-duddy." Jane gets it, and says, "Like our brother Volodya who's been a young fuddy-duddy for years!" Anne chimes in, "Yeah, he used to drive his '67 Caddy a few blocks just for cigarettes." But Jane has noticed a change in their older brother since his good friends encouraged him to join them on hikes in and around the Hollywood Hills. She says, "It's unbelievable. Now he's out riding his bike almost every day. He sparkles."

How does this rule translate into daily life? We all calculate how old we will be when we pay off the mortgage. We all notice that we're stiffer in the morning than when we hit the pillow at night. And some of us wonder how whiskers suddenly appear on our chin in the morning. Let's face it, we all know that time marches on. But Age Is Irrelevant tells us to stop putting age into the equation of how we want to live our lives. Our mind and body wind down with time, but this doesn't mean you can't wind them back up, just like you do with the clock on the mantelpiece.

Yoga calls the vital energy of the mind-body system *prana*. You can restore this energy in various ways: being physically active, eating nourishing food and keeping good company. But you must take action. And that is sometimes the hardest part.

Once we hit a certain age, we invent all kinds of excuses for being out of shape. "If it's in the fridge, I'll eat the leftover pizza after dinner." "When I go to bed late, I skip my two-mile run in the morning." "I'm in my forties, it's the hormones." Does this sound familiar?

"That's not being old," Jane says, "that's not taking responsibility for yourself!" She adds, "Our mother didn't keep up her Jack LaLanne routine because of kids and her career. Why not be fit and healthy as we grow older?" Anne agrees, "Our father was a prime example of fitness, even in his eighties. Every morning he did his jumping jacks, deep knee bends and scissor kicks as he watched the news."

This rule says we can be fit at any age. Even if this is a monumental challenge for some of you out there, we encourage you, Dear Reader, to uphold this rule of Rome to the best of your abilities.

Jane tells her story, "When I first moved to Los Angeles, I had my share of anxiety and money worries, and I was not in my twenties anymore. I wasn't in my thirties either. I'd tell myself, 'Go for a walk.' I knew if I just got out and walked around the block, things would change for the better. I'd still have problems, but they wouldn't weigh so heavily." So when you're brooding, go walk around the block: look at the trees, listen to the birds, breathe. Then get back to your worries and woes. They're not going anywhere; they'll still be in your in-box. Anne asks, "What does this have to do with Age Is Irrelevant?" Jane answers, "I digress. Bottom line, exercise!"

Have you noticed that we as a society put age limitations on learning? You will hear people say, "You can't master an instrument after high school" or "I wish I had learned another language when I was young." Anne has always thwarted such naysaying: "If I want to take up farming, I will farm. I have learned to use a jackhammer and a chainsaw. And currently I'm learning Sanskrit, sort of." Jane says encouragingly, "It's so much fun to be a beginner. I really wanted to learn the guitar to accompany the songs I wrote. Though I admit I wanted to throw the guitar out the window many a time." Anne asks, "Did you really?" Jane exclaims, "Oh, God, yes! It was hard. My fingers hurt. But that was just beginner's blues. You get past it and then it's fun." After six months of practicing a little each day and studying with a gifted teacher, Jane started performing at open mics, family parties and around the campfire. Anne has learned how to put up drywall and do masonry while renovating a couple of stone houses.

Have you also noticed that sometimes age is an excuse for limiting the fun you can have? You're too old for this. You're too old for that. Dear Reader, the spirit is ageless. Anne remembers walking in downtown Washington, D.C., and spotting somebody skipping down the sidewalk amidst a throng of gray suits and trench coats. It was their father. She says, "He was an emeritus professor for goodness' sakes. And he had a friend with him trying to keep up!" Jane smiles and winks, "Our Dad got more fun and youthful as he got older."

She follows his youthful example in her own ways, saying, "A couple of years ago, I was hiking with friends up to the top of Malibu Canyon and there was a beautiful tree with branches on it that were like parallel bars at the gym. I wanted to climb that tree even though my friends thought it was dangerous. After all, only kids climb trees. I thought about it for a second, but I did it anyway because I like climbing trees! And let me tell you, I will never forget the view of Malibu and the Pacific from up there."

Anne chimes in, "That reminds me of when we were on Pasquale's island and I was alone at the rocky private beach. After taking a skinny dip I went rock climbing naked." Jane exclaims, "What, no shoes?" Anne corrects herself, "I had my Keens on. I climbed to a bluff overlooking the sea with nothing between me and Africa." Jane ponders this, then inquires, "Is this a new definition of bushwhacking?"

Dear Reader, let's move on to the subject of clothes, shall we? Young people often judge older people on what they wear. Why, when you hit a certain age, do clothes have to look a certain way: drabber colors, less stylish cuts? Jane confesses, "Maybe I pick up on that frequency because our mother never wore anything sexy, *ever*. When she wasn't wearing her nursing clothes, it was mostly muumuu time, unless there was a wedding."

The sisters *pause,* remembering their mother's seemingly eternal red housedress. Anne adds, "In the summer, she'd tie it above her knees." The sisters giggle. But Jane, a student of the Roman Seven, states clearly, "I prefer the example of Sharon Stone. She wears patent-leather thigh-high boots, and she's *over sixty*." This rule has to do with owning your look. Wear big glasses or shave your head, swagger in Converse sneakers or strut your stuff in five-inch heels, if that's your thing. Age Is Irrelevant.

How does this rule apply when in Rome? When Anne and Jane were in Rome, they strolled the Piazza Navona by night, admiring its famous Bernini fountain. In ancient times, the piazza was a grassy field for sporting events. Caesar Augustus erected an obelisk there, a trophy he had brought from Egypt. Bernini, the greatest architect in Europe 350 years ago, found the obelisk under the ground during construction of the piazza and topped his fountain with it. Anne and Jane enjoyed the fountain's cool mist while they imagined Roman athletes with chiseled torsos thrusting heavy things about.

After their historical musings, Anne and Jane left the piazza and wandered into the pulsing atmosphere of a crowded hipster discotheque. That's when Marco noticed them and came right up to Jane and offered to buy her a cocktail. Jane was wearing her hot pink dress and new strappy shoes. Marco's slightly receding hairline and gentlemanly manner were decoys for the handsome, young graduate student that he was. They danced and talked and he stayed by Jane's side until she agreed to go see Rome by night with him. She returned with Anne to their hotel just long enough to grab a toothbrush, then she jumped into a Fiat with three Italian grad students and went gallivanting into the night. Meanwhile, Anne practiced Italian with her favorite desk clerk before turning in. When Jane returned the next morning in time for breakfast, she recounted her hot steamy night and something about juicy peaches.

Age Is Irrelevant is saying that if you want a relationship there are no age restrictions. And what some would dismiss as a one-night stand, others would see as an unexpected Roman gift, all wrapped up with a bow on top. While on this subject, the sisters seek more wisdom from their brilliant and witty diplomat friend, Janet. Cool as a cucumber, like her green eyes, Janet states with absolute certainty: "Of course, Age Is Irrelevant! Personally, I always found older men more stimulating. Twenty years or more was fine. I have very little experience with younger men. I rarely met one who was interesting to me. They don't have the classical education."

When it comes to relationships, it's not age that matters, but the spirit of the people and the abundance of life and love shared between them. Remember Chloe, our elegant cougar? She and Max are twenty years apart and after three years of dating, they took the plunge and moved in together.

Janet, a fount of pragmatism, makes this recommendation: "If you want to get married and have a partner for life, it is better to marry a younger man. In terms of the actuarial tables, women live longer."

Yes, women live longer, and in light of that, this rule also says: *Own the lines!* We mean the wrinkles. Jane sighs, "I'm looking at this face of mine and trying to get used to it. I'm still pursuing an acting career; I'll just play older parts when I break through."

May we talk about grooming as an exception here? Jane reminds us, "Age Is Irrelevant as long as you groom: no ear hairs, no nose hairs, no chin hairs! Because when you age up and you don't groom, age *is* relevant." Anne questions, "Maybe this rule matters less when you're seventy?" Jane replies, "I'd say 'no' to that. Wrinkles and arthritis may be part of life, but the spirit doesn't age. *We* let things age *us*. Dad lived to eighty-three, skipping down the sidewalks, and he groomed!" Whether you prefer an older partner with a classical education or a younger one as a cougar snack, Age Is Irrelevant.

We ask the great centurion, Arianne, to weigh in on this rule when it comes to moving to a new place and starting over. "When I retired fifteen years ago at the age of sixty-seven, people thought I was too old to move to a foreign country," she tells us. "Well, I moved to Nice. My apartment is from the 1920s. My friend Alain is my tango teacher. He's also a first-rate craftsman. He gutted my kitchen and created the most amazing space. The walls are marine blue, the counter is made out of Brazilian slate, the backsplash is made of brick. It was like his art project."

Since moving to the Riviera, Arianne reads a lot, walks a lot and nourishes her passion for the tango. "I wasn't physically very flexible before learning the tango," she says. "I love Alain. He gave me a lesson and I remembered everything he taught me. Since then, he comes to my apartment for class and sometimes it lasts three hours. We take breaks and have drinks. If I were forty years younger, I'd go for him, but I'm better off having him as my teacher."

What about sex as you get older? Dear Reader, you may be asking yourself, "Am I bored? Am I gay?

Should I go out and buy a hot piece of lingerie and become a sea creature in green sequins rather than curl up in bed and read Edith Wharton's *The House of Mirth?* Is it okay if I prefer reading about other people's dalliances or watching them on Netflix rather than having them myself?"

Anne's friend Sarah, a florist, speaks frankly about this challenge. She has been part of a loving couple for years and yet remains puzzled by this subject: "My partner and I have always enjoyed having people over for dinner. It's fun and genuine. I love decorating and cooking. Then when our guests go home and we're a little tipsy, instead of being romantic we say, 'Let's watch the news.'" Anne asks in a friendly way, "Can't you take his hand and lead him to the bedroom?" Sarah chuckles, "No, that doesn't happen. Our sex life needs to be resurrected, like Jesus."

The sisters ponder the following: It seems that in the natural course of life non-sexual aspects of a loving relationship will at some point have more value. So, does this imply that there will come a time when sex doesn't matter as much? Our seasoned friend Janet assents, but with this caveat, "Unless you live in France, where women in their sixties have twice as much sex as they do in this country."

Vive la France! Or, as they say in Rome, *Gallia vivat!*

PRACTICE

Age Is Irrelevant is a state of mind that needs to be cultivated. Try new things that are unconventional for your age: climb a tree or play Twister with friends. Be spontaneous. Say yes more often. Be daring. And we don't mean rob a bank. Wear a T-shirt and thigh-high boots like Sharon Stone. It might not be your cup of tea in the end, but you're bound to surprise yourself. It's fun to try new things. Practice keeps you young at heart and keeps the spirit shining. Learn a language or an instrument, start a new sport like mixed martial arts or pole dancing. Try skiing! You can always learn on the bunny hill—you don't have to go down the black diamond slopes. "I go skiing every four or five years," says Jane, "even though I turn blue and my nose runs."

Here are a few reminders to help ensure a *sex-cessful* time at any age. On date nights conserve your energy for the evening. Brush your teeth and gargle. Light candles. Put silk sheets on the bed and jump in: showered, shaved and naked. Age Is Irrelevant.

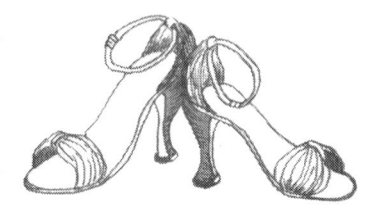

RULE V

TRUST THE HEAT

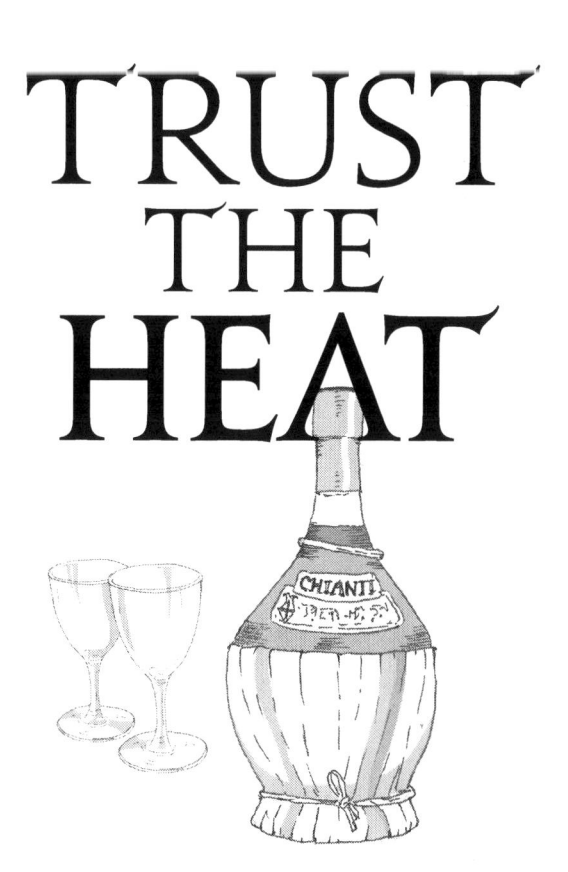

RULE V

TRUST THE HEAT

Science of Heat; Different Heat-Forms; Karla and Ruis; Larissa and Johan; Bombshell Heat; "Something To Talk About"; Miriam and the Norwegian; Jennifer and the Professor; Jane and Keith; Mom and Dad's humor; Veronica and Frankie; Bruce's Rule

Heat, in Roman parlance, is attraction, chemistry. People have written about Heat for centuries in poems, songs, novels and movies. It's two people who just wanna jump each other's bones. Go for a roll in the hay. Be thrown up against a wall and kissed. Flipped over like a filet mignon in a cast-iron skillet. Sizzle, sizzle, hot, hot. You can't think straight. You can't stop thinking about that person.

Let's see what Science has to say. Out in nature, when something like a campfire emits heat, people around the blaze absorb the warmth. What is happening there? The hot logs give off electromagnetic radiation which is absorbed by you. Your clothes and skin molecules then vibrate at the same frequency as the hot embers in the fire. This is how you warm up. Science also says that there is no absolute zero temperature in the universe. *Everything* is giving off heat. Even the atoms out in interstellar space give off heat, and it's darn cold out there.

Let's face it, Science may be interesting, but we all want steamy examples of Heat, don't we? However, Dear Reader, this is a vast and complex subject, so let's first break down the concept into a few of its many forms. The goal here is to help you make wise decisions and avoid some disasters in relationships. Trust the Heat can lead to a mutually satisfying one-night stand, a romance that segues into a friendship, an encounter with *Groomzilla*, or it just may lead to a lifelong love. Be warned, this subject is not for beginners.

We briefly list below the Heat terminology you will need so you can better master this rule.

- Self-Generated Heat
- Collaborative Heat
- Bombshell Heat
- Short-Term Heat
- Long-Term Heat à la Carte
- Long-Term Heat with Love

We begin with Self-Generated Heat. This is a tricky Heat form. It can be attraction mixed with longing for a relationship, *any* relationship! Or it can be that one person in the couple is delusional about the reciprocity of Heat. We all know what this feels like: "I'm more into him than he's into me." Your partner has only one foot in the relationship. This Heat is not to be trusted.

Jane's young friend Karla, a bouncy and dimpled young actress, had just moved to Manhattan and was sharing a mouse-infested walk-up in Chinatown. While she was still starry-eyed, a magnificent Latin popped up as a match on Bumble. Ruis was the kind of young man that seems to only own bathing suits and makes your friends drool all over his Instagram. He said to Karla in a sexy form of English, "I'm being honest with you. I want to get married," and asked her to move in with him. Karla was overjoyed and called Jane with the news. Jane's boyfriend, a former marine, shared his wisdom on these star-crossed lovers: "That guy's a fuckin' musclehead. Sure, you can't judge a book by its cover, but don't fucking fall in love with a meathead who's looking for a U.S. bride. You have to go beyond the physical aspects—it's character that's important!"

The first wave of COVID was raging in New York at the time, so Karla decided to go wait it out back home in LA and think over Ruis' proposition. During that time he phoned her daily with declarations of his love for her. She felt major Heat, indeed. After a few weeks she decided to fly back to the besieged Big Apple and move in with *the man she loved*. She thought the Fates were smiling upon her.

The Three Roman Fates chitchatted as they wove Karla's destiny on their loom:

Nona said, wryly, "It's as clear as the nose on my face, he's only after a green card."

Decima lamented, "She's gonna get her heart broken."

Morta raised her eyes to the heavens and sighed, "Oy vey!"

Soon after Karla moved in, Ruis started putting pressure on her to marry him. She told him she needed more time and asked, "Don't you want to talk more and have a deeper understanding of each other first?" Did you guess, Dear Reader, that he did not? Instead, he became verbally abusive, so Karla got a hotel room and called Jane. She had left most of her things in Ruis' apartment and was afraid to go back alone. In search of a solution, Jane called her Jersey buddy, Deanna, a valiant centurion who causes many to tremble in their boots. Her no-nonsense response was, "No problem. Tell him to come on over, I'll have my Glock waiting for him." Deanna made some calls to law enforcement and they made sure Karla got her belongings.

Heat is a double-edged sword. It gives warmth to life, but it can also burn. Use caution, Dear Reader. Self-Generated Heat got Karla big-time trouble. But as a centurion you learn your lessons, pick up the pieces and move on. As we write this we are pleased to say that Karla is happily single and thriving in the Big Apple.

Now let's see what happens when Heat enters a working relationship. Anne's former co-worker, Larissa, a forty-something corporate manager, had befriended Johan, her Frankfurt-based cohort who was tall, attractive and well-perched on the executive ladder in a sister company. Long-distance texting gave intimacy to their enjoyable work-play relationship. Larissa thought there was Heat. After several months of increasingly chummy happy hours in cities throughout Europe, she emailed Johan, asking if he wanted to take it to the next level. She imagined gondola rides, the Eiffel Tower, champagne and flower picnics. She felt Heat. But Johan's response was cold, *ice caps*. He sent her a lengthy email describing his management style and his affinity for corporate power and praising Larissa for being such a stellar business partner. Dear Reader, Johan didn't show the slightest reaction to the Heat Larissa had been self-generating.

Jane exclaims, "That's why we've been writing *The Seven Roman Rules!* We don't want relationships to turn into a bore fest." She imagines Larissa penning this response:

> "Dearest Johan, thank you for sharing your deepest thoughts. Your email sent me into a drooling coma as my head dropped onto my laptop. It allowed me to fall asleep, peacefully. I didn't have to pop a Benadryl to knock me out. By the time I raised my forehead from the keyboard, I had typed ten pages of G's and H's. I realize that our relationship was just a whole lot of nothingburger. I appreciate your truth and rhetoric. It added a brick in my shoe instead of a spring in my step."

Who has not been in Larissa's position? Jane sums up the situation thusly, "It wasn't amateur hour for her, it was just Self-Generated Heat." After a *pause*, Anne suggests, "Maybe Larissa has Collaborative Heat with her colleague and she can salvage that aspect of the relationship?" Jane remarks, "Oh, that's one of my favorite Heat forms!" Anne adds, "Yes, and it's sustainable. It can be generated in a work environment where two colleagues enjoy great chemistry and synergy." Jane says, "Let's share this with Larissa so she can move on from Johan."

We admit that Trust the Heat is one of the hardest rules to master. There are occasional pitfalls but with practice you can identify them quickly and move on. The sisters decide to consult with expert centurions about this rule. They subpoena their diplomat friend, Janet. She has this caveat, "Trust the Heat as long as he's available or interested." With a calm demeanor and steady green eyes she confesses: "I once worked at the Defense Department for a program director who was drop-dead gorgeous, the son of a famous U.N. diplomat. Such a presence! When a senior female colleague noticed my passion for him, I confessed to her that I was going to throw myself down in front of him the next time we were alone. My esteemed colleague was amused and said, 'Just like every other woman who works in this office. By the way, his wife is a sexy knockout.'"

What Janet describes is a form of Heat that is explosive and omnidirectional. Science would call this phenomenon a singularity. We call it Bombshell Heat. Think Marilyn Monroe. Think Tina Turner. Think Brad Pitt. They're all sexy knockouts. The opposite sex becomes hot and bothered by them, even if they're just folding laundry.

Nell, a family friend from our parents' generation, had her own view of this Heat form. She used to say, "There's no such thing as unrequited love." As it turns out, Nell had Bombshell Heat, so she never experienced unrequited love. She was a sexy knockout well into middle age.

Dear Reader, the above examples of Heat are common, but you only have Roman Heat when it's mutual. Let's go back to the Science, the mutual vibrations of two bodies at a distance. With Roman Heat, when you ask, does he feel the way I do? The answer is, Hell, yeah! If you feel the attraction, it is there. *Trust it!* And it is highly likely that other people around you will notice it. Just like in the song "Something To Talk About" by the honorable centurion Bonnie Raitt. She's talkin' 'bout a vibration that two people share. Bonnie tells it like it is: If you're feeling it, he's feeling it. So what do you do when you experience Roman Heat? Trust it. With every ounce of your being.

Let us now consider the Roman Heat form, Short-Term Heat. This is great for encounters that may be sizzling-hot out of the gate, and therefore perfect for a romp, but will cool down fast. These relationships may help when you're in transition or weathering the storms of life, like having a buoy on rough seas. This form of Heat has nothing to do with whether a person will be a good partner for you in the long run. In fact, he may be a terrible partner for you.

Miriam, an art gallery curator from Queens, shared her story: "The Norwegian looked like Johnny Depp.

He was buying a falafel sandwich on the street in SoHo. I said, Hi. Who wouldn't say hello to Johnny Depp? With that musketeer beard he looked older than he was. He asked me to walk with him, so I did. I'd never done that before. Then he offered to buy me a beer and said it was the least he could do to thank me. After making out in the bar, we made out in the stairwell on the way up to his apartment. There was a lot of passion and flinging each other against the walls. I still don't know how old he was, but I remember seeing a diploma on one of the walls and thinking, 'I hope this is a graduate school diploma.' Who puts their diploma on their wall? Kids do. He was a Stanford graduate, but it smelled like a locker room in there, clothes, computers and gadgets everywhere. He was very responsible, though, and had condoms in a little tin, like a first aid kit, which I had never seen before. We hooked up until the tin was empty. Then I met my soul mate, Kevin. He and I are each other's best friend. However, it isn't like the Norwegian flinging me up against the wall. He's still out there if I want him. It's like keeping an emergency bottle of Bordeaux after you quit drinking."

Let's remain in New York City for a slightly longer tale of Short-Term Heat. Sometimes a passionate Heat experience transforms, awkwardly, into a lackluster relationship.

Jane shares her story. She met her ex-boyfriend, Keith, at the Neighborhood Playhouse on the Upper East Side. "He was tall and slim like a handsome prince, a playwright in a tweed jacket," she says. "There sure was Heat! He asked me to dinner before we left the venue." Anne wonders, "That relationship lasted a while. You produced plays together. What happened to the Heat?"

Jane recalls, "He suggested I move in with him, so I did. We were in love, after all. And, heck, it was New York, I could save money!" Anne recollects their compact one-bedroom on 96th: "It was definitely his space, not yours. And there was his anxiety." Jane agrees, "Yes, a little Woody Allen."

She continues, "His work desk was in the bedroom, as well as a huge bookshelf jammed with books and plays, where nothing *ever* moved. And everything in the apartment was centered and square, even the coffee table. There were no other shapes. I felt trapped, in the apartment and in my life with him. Did I tell you that after three and a half years, I felt that bookshelf caving in on me? I kept thinking, maybe I should cover it. Instead, I withdrew from the relationship. Now, I recognize that we had Short-Term Heat that fizzled. It wasn't enough to sustain a partnership."

There is another Roman Heat form that is felt at the start of a relationship and lasts for a very long time. However, it doesn't necessarily lead to love and partnership. We call this Long-Term Heat à la Carte. It can be *light fare* if you don't want to be in a committed relationship: "I'll have the salad instead of the cheeseburger with fries." But, more specifically, it is Heat between two people that, unlike the heat of a campfire, doesn't go away, even after many years. You can throw water on the coals and make them smolder, but as soon as you blow on them, *whoosh*, a hot red flame dances up out of those embers that never went cold. It is a wonderful phenomenon, even if it never warms to a union.

Jane says, "Let's get Jennifer's testimony. Her Long-Term Heat is like a Netflix miniseries!" The sisters Zoom Jennifer, Anne's old college friend, an athletic strawberry blonde with porcelain skin. Jane takes notes as Jennifer tells her intricate story of Long-Term Heat à la Carte with a dash of bad timing. "I met the Professor in London during my first year in graduate school. He was a much older man, a hotshot in his field. He would pop into my office and get my attention with witty jokes. I had to play it cool because I shared the office with my then-boyfriend." It was a conundrum. Anne and Jane listen attentively. "What made things worse," Jennifer shares, "was that the Professor was single and charming, with curly black locks."

There was plenty of Heat, and age was clearly irrelevant, but they did not blow on those coals. A year later, Jennifer was single and decided to go on holiday to the banks of Lac Léman, in Évian, France, where spring water gushes from Alpine granite. She describes how they rekindled the Heat: "The Professor called and said he was close by, attending a conference in Geneva. So I invited him to come visit Évian. He said, 'I will meet you tonight without fail.'" Jane looks up from her notepad, to catch every word. "We couldn't keep our hands off each other. At one point he said in his sexy British accent, 'You've got the right genetic material. You could have my baby!' I felt a tug. I couldn't tell if he was teasing or not. Then he confessed that he was tied up in a new relationship. So we had an enjoyable romp, and then we said goodbye."

Still, the Heat in those embers did not die. A few years later Jennifer was doing research at Cambridge. She was now in a relationship, albeit a lukewarm one. Imagine her delight when she spotted the Professor striding across the Trinity College green in a black teaching gown and jauntily angled cap.

This time he was single and asked to meet up. Jennifer recollects, "I went with him to a private dinner at the headmaster's mansion. It was a fun, memorable meal. After dinner, we snuck around the place, a Henry VIII–esque castle, full of chambers and corridors. We wanted to jump each other's bones, but we behaved ourselves." They had to chuck water on the coals.

The embers stayed lit for the next ten years. Then one day, the Professor called Jennifer out of the blue. This time they were both married. She was living near Paris with her husband and extended family. He was living in London with his American wife and young son. He asked if he could visit since he was in Paris for a conference. Jennifer invited him for dinner, cooked a festive family meal and everybody enjoyed the company of the witty Professor. Especially Jennifer. There was still Long-Term Heat à la Carte.

This rule says savor the Heat; you can always be *friends with no benefits.* It's a tango. Here is the thing about Heat—you touch it and it sizzles. And it's still hot twenty years later. "Talk about renewable energy," Jane says. "That's electricity without the solar panels or the wind farms!" Anne adds, "I think that's the takeaway with Heat. Trust it. Have it. Get as much as you can in a lifetime."

Jane muses on the man's perspective when it comes to Heat. "They'll jump on anything. They can't distinguish. It's just sex for them, isn't it? Or is it?" Anne responds, "Yes, that's true for many men. But for those who are looking for a long-term relationship, Heat is not just about sex." Read on, Dear Reader.

What do most of us really want? Long-Term Heat with Love! It is a rare occurrence in nature. This Heat is like a well-stoked fire that warms the relationship over the years. It gets turned into love that is expressed as patience, tolerance, friendship, respect. We see this in some marriages that last a lifetime where elderly couples still hold hands. Jane observes, "They may be old and gray but they must've had Heat." Anne utters, reverently, "And they still do."

Anne and Jane pause. Anne wonders, "Who do we know who still has this kind of Heat in their relationship after years together?" Jane responds, "Yeah, because neither of us has hit a home run in that department." Their parents were not a good example, although with eight children there must have been some Heat.

Anne holds up a straight-faced mask and recites their mother's one and only joke, a favorite of their father's: "Two spinsters are watching a hen cross the road. She's being chased by a rooster. Suddenly, the hen runs in front of a car and gets killed. 'She'd rather die!' exclaims one of the spinsters as the other nods in agreement."

Jane holds up a grinning mask and intones in their father's thick Russian accent: "Your mother and I can skip our anniversary this year. We celebrated our fortieth last year. We can wait another forty years."

The sisters lower their masks. They are indeed stumped about finding examples of Long-Term Heat with Love. Anne wonders, "Such relationships are steeped in legend. Maybe we need to seek the testimony of a centurion." Jane agrees, "I know, Veronica Velazquez! She is funny, confident and always looking sexy! Let's Zoom her."

Veronica and her husband, Frankie, met in college, have two teenagers and have been happily married for twenty-eight years. Veronica sits at her kitchen table and describes the Heat with Frankie:

"The day we met at an audition for our college production of *The Music Man*, we both felt the attraction. But we were already in relationships. The director noticed that we had great chemistry. He cast us and we fell in love in the wings. Once we finally started dating, there was major attraction. We had so much fun just being together. We didn't even have sex until months later. And then he'd run over to my dorm during his forty-five-minute lunch breaks and I'd be wearing a goddess costume. *That* was his lunch. I knew he was the right guy for me because I'm gay-friendly and he accepted my friends. I even suggested he explore that side of himself, as I had done, but he never tried. A girlfriend of mine, who's bi, once said I have the best of both worlds: Frankie is a heterosexual man, but his emotional sensitivity is similar to a woman's. He remembers things, like our first date when we had pizza and a Diet Coke. A year later, I came home from work and there was a Diet Coke and a pizza with some candles on it sitting on the table. Our anniversary dinner! He's a Renaissance man. He cooks. He cleans. He is attentive in bed and always takes care of me first."

Minerva, Diana and Venus have been listening in.

Minerva exclaims, "Foreplay ... there's a word!"

Diana asks, rhetorically, "Does that belong anywhere in this rule book?"

Venus asserts, "There can never be enough."

Anne asks Veronica the question that has been on her mind, "How do you fan the flames of Heat during a long marriage?" Veronica thinks for a moment. "We didn't do date nights. We didn't take care of the Heat enough. A long time would pass between our romps. The kids are older, finally! I'm definitely hornier now than I used to be. On my birthday, Frankie put candles up in the bedroom and massaged me naked, and other stuff. It was really sexy."

Veronica lowers her voice because the kids are around, "A friend of mine, a sex counselor, said it's good to have sex once a week. I'm thinking it would be good to try toys and watch a porn movie together. Something tasteful." Anne suggests, "How about an *Emmanuelle* movie? They are French classics from the sexual liberation era." Veronica enthusiastically jots down the suggestion, saying, "Honestly, I'm ready for him to be less sensitive. Throw me against the wall. Frankie is someone who will give things a try, so I remind him, 'I want you to tie me up.' He said we don't have a lock on the bedroom door. 'Well, too bad,' I said. 'If the kids don't knock, they may see their mom's ass in the air.'"

Veronica laughs heartily. Then she *pauses* and reflects, "I think couples fall in and out of love during the course of the relationship. Luckily, we never fall out of love at the same time. Sometimes, I look at him and I want to run. But we are life partners and I know I can wait out those times."

Anne and Jane are spellbound, hanging on to every word Veronica has shared. Her relationship is one that helps to define love as devotion, tenderness and affection. This, combined with laughter, good sex and space for individual growth, is the gold standard of Long-Term Heat with Love. The sisters say goodbye and as the Zoom session ends, they watch the great centurion feed her shaggy white rescue dog.

Do the odds seem to be one in a million that you will have a Long-Term Heat with Love relationship? Anne and Jane reach out to an elder, Bruce, a learned comedy writer. He shares this wisdom: "The reasons why Heat lasts with some and not others is always a mystery. Why Ellen said yes to me fifty-three years ago was a mystery to me then and it is now. I've always said that when the gods hand you the greatest gift you will ever get, your only job is not to screw it up. I'm surrounded by couples who have been married as long or longer than Ellen and I. This is my observation, and I pass it on for what it's worth: The men in all of these marriages *cherish* their wives. For me, that's where the Heat is. For all the ladies out there, call it *Bruce's Rule*. If the guy doesn't cherish you, move on."

Minerva and Diana raise their goblets and toast: "To Bruce's Rule!"

Venus nods and adds: "To Ellen, a wife who champions her husband!"

PRACTICE

Short-Term and Self-Generated Heat can be fun and may boost your mojo, but they can also lead to confusion and have unpleasant outcomes. Trust the Heat, but when you realize that it isn't for you, move on. Why? Because most of us are looking for Long-Term Heat with Love. If you need to cool off from a Heat interest, do something that will distract you: go out with friends, order a pizza, jump in a glacier lake.

We want to be wise in the application of this rule and make better choices. Jane suggests, "We should have training in high school on how to be in a relationship, learning patience and tolerance *and* how to brush your teeth and take a shower before date night." Anne agrees, "As juniors we could learn how to put the toothpaste cap back on and lower the toilet lid. As seniors we could learn how to be more direct and appreciative." The sisters think how great we'd all be at adult relationships after such training.

Women of Roman lineage have to get comfortable with Heat so they can understand their power. Anne points out, "You don't need to go to third base." Jane adds, "Yeah, if you can stand the Heat, you can stay in the kitchen. Warm your hands by the stove, so to speak. No judgments here." Women are intuitive and know more often than not when there is Heat. Anne advises, "But you may have to open the kitchen door so that the guy knows it's okay to pursue. A nod and a smile may be necessary."

Take a Heat reading with him. It doesn't mean you have to act on it. Indeed, that could be a bad move, like Karla's experience with Ruis. And your friends will tell you so. But if you're up for a romp, then act on it, safely. Or if there is potential for a relationship, don't feel you have to run from base to base, especially if you think that person might be *the one*. If that is the case, then Trust the Heat means he will wait, and that may be a good thing for the relationship. You might just hit a home run like Veronica!

Warning: In a relationship, you may get lonely or bored and say to yourself, "I need a hobby, I need to travel, I need sex, I need a new streaming platform." In the end, Dear Reader, if you want to have a Long-Term Heat relationship, then you have to fan the flames. Nothing beats Heat with your partner. Things may be on low Heat at times, barely a simmer. At which point you may say, "Let's see what we can cook up tonight."

RULE VI

CARPE
TIEMPO

RULE VI

CARPE TIEMPO
(WASTE NO TIME)

Under the arch; François Mitterrand; The Pinch; Trang's baby; Science and time; Arianne's ritual; Bongos in Rome; Laugh until you pee; Tim and Becky; Party like it's 1999

What is time from a Roman perspective? Picture the following: We're two sisters strolling by night through the beautiful, illuminated ruins of the ancient city of Rome. We pass under a gigantic stone arch that we guess to be at least 500 years old. Boy, are we wrong! After consulting our trusted Siri, we find out it was built in 300 BC. That's more than 2,300 years old. Whaaaaat? We can't even wrap our heads around that amount of time. People, namely slaves, spent their whole lives building that F-ing arch! What happened to them? What happened to their stories, to their dogs and cats? How did they have fun? We know they had sports and culture, Aesop's fables and the like. How did we get from then to now? It's mind blowing when you start to think about it.

We pause to reflect. What are we doing with our lives? Well, at present we're strollin' in Rome, lookin' at ruins and about to drink some wine. A strapping waiter is waving to us, gesturing toward an outdoor table under a deep-green awning. But what about the bigger picture? How can we look at the passage of time and make it add up to something? Are we just coasting? Are we wasting time? This rule says do the opposite: Waste No Time. Or, in Latin parlance, *Carpe Tiempo*. Another way to translate this is: Seize the dynamic of time.

Jane recollects Edward Morehouse, a seasoned Herbert Berghof Studio acting teacher in New York City, who asked his class, "Who has a scene to do?" When her fellow students looked around, shrugging their shoulders, he admonished them, "Gotta get busy or you'll waste your life." Jane adds, "There was plenty of resonance in what he said. He didn't have to shout."

François Mitterrand, one of France's shortest and most virile presidents, had a wonderful concept of time, *"Il faut laisser du temps au temps."* In English, this translates jauntily as, "You have to *make* the time in order to *have* the time." Jane says, "Yeah, it's like making a basket full of time. If I wake up at 6 a.m. instead of 7 a.m.,

I get an extra hour to journal, do yoga, meditate, plan my day in an unrushed way and then eat breakfast."

Carpe Tiempo is not about frenetic over-activity. Some may find that life is made richer by taking it slow. The Roman example is fitting. Everybody there is beautiful, but maybe a source of that beauty is their relaxed, confident quality. They exude a sexiness and dress in a colorful, playful way. Even the food is sexy in Italy; everything tastes better. Why is that? Italians take time with their meals. Imagine a simple and delicious lunch of spinach and potato soup with wine and crusty bread, then a stroll through enchanted gardens strewn with ruins of Corinthian columns, where one may hear a string quartet.

Jane evokes a concept of time from her pre-Roman days called *The Pinch*. "I used to think I could only take one week of vacation during the summer. So on day seven, I'd take a night flight home, take a shower and change, and then head straight to work in the afternoon. You know, *The Pinch*. I didn't think I could justify staying away longer to my boss or my boyfriend." These days, after rigorously practicing this Roman rule, Jane takes two weeks of vacation. There's no rush. "It's *Carpe Tiempo* without pinching," Anne remarks approvingly.

How about taking the time to start a family? Anne Zooms her friend Trang, a successful social media marketer who made the time to stay home with her baby girl. Anne remarks, "Career women get stuck thinking they can't possibly do what you did." Trang sweeps a strand of long hair from her forehead as she bounces one-year-old Lucy on her lap. "The hardest thing I had to do when the baby came was turn down work," she says. "Basically, I told my clients, you'll have to get used to this for a while. We've been living month-to-month from my income and my husband Antonio's graduate student loans, but thanks to Lucy, I'm much more relaxed about money." Anne remarks, "The love for your baby makes those oxytocins that help you float over obstacles you would have stressed about." Trang responds, "That's exactly what happens. This is my job. And she is such a joy! Motherhood has enriched my life more than I could have imagined. Antonio and I are so grateful."

Anne asks, "What would you say to women approaching forty and hesitating between career and motherhood?" Trang responds, "Jeez! You can always work. I put in extra hours all the time. But when can you have a one-year-old bringing joy and laughter into your life? I wish I had had more confidence about doing this and hadn't been so terrified pre-baby. Now we're looking forward to doing more traveling with Lucy.

She already had her first plane trip to Chicago and we'll see her grandparents in Italy as soon as we can."

People can play hard, work hard, love hard, and also have that joie de vivre, that enjoyment of life, which includes playtime with your baby.

In order to *Carpe Tiempo* you may have to go a bit overboard compared to your norm, to break out of a blah routine and strike a new balance. Arianne, the great tango-dancing centurion living in Nice, has a joyous routine for seizing the dynamic of time. She explains, "I have this little technique where I have my alarm set every hour. And every hour I dance. Or I sing if it gets late, something like Patsy Cline, so I don't disturb the neighbors."

As the sisters stood under that colossal arch of glistening marble, they realized there was a whole different concept of time out there. Roman time is about feasting on experiences. By doing something that excites and challenges you and feeds your soul, you are expanding time exponentially. How is this possible?

Here's an equation:

Desire + Action + Experiences = Time to the nth degree

Science makes everybody perk up and pay attention. What is another scientific concept of time? Physicists talk about a thing they call space-time, which basically means that time is just as fillable as space.

Our lives can overflow with sights, sounds, smells and tastes that delight and fill the spirit as we pay more attention to the simplest of experiences; listening to the birds chirp, smelling the sweetness of a rose, tasting homemade *nocciola* gelato with a dollop of fresh whipped cream, we sense we are living life to the fullest.

The Chorus, in unison, inquires with delight: "How do we *Carpe Tiempo* when in Rome?"

Imagine the sun beginning to set over the Colosseum, people of all ages coming out to stroll in the cool evening air and a happy, chatty crowd beginning to gather at the restaurant terraces. Some people may think the ultimate experience is to go to the Vatican and watch the pope wave from the balcony … and that's okay. A different experience, such as dancing the tango at 2 a.m. with the owner of a restaurant on the Piazza San Marco while his buddy plays the bongos, could be equally memorable. What matters is that you pack your day with fun, food and adventure when you travel—to Rome or anywhere.

"Sleep when you're dead, right?" Jane suggests. "When in Rome …" Anne agrees.

The Chorus nods in approbation.

The sisters begin to giggle about one of their nights in Rome. They remember enjoying a final glass of Chianti at a beautiful outdoor restaurant terrace. The normally busy piazza took on a mysterious beauty at that late hour. The restaurant owner announced that he was closing and politely suggested that the sisters join him and his friend inside. He generously poured icy *limoncello* for everyone, and soon pulled out a guitar and began to sing. His friend would not be outdone and joined in on the bongos. To continue the entertainment without waking the neighborhood, the owner invited everyone downstairs into the vaulted and extraordinarily kitsch dining room. Plastic begonias festooned faux marble columns, and a wall-sized photo of the island of Capri created a backdrop for an improvised tango with Anne, one of those plastic begonias held between her teeth.

Some of the experiences you create or pounce on may not be the smartest ones. Like when Anne ventured into the restaurant's broom closet with the bongo player after doing the tango. But if you *Carpe Tiempo*, you will most likely have a life filled with great memories. These will feed your soul during long winter months, or while you raise your kids, or while you eat your sandwich in front of your computer at work.

So, what exactly happened in the broom closet with Anne and the bongo player? What took place we leave to your imagination, Dear Reader. It will probably be more exciting than what actually transpired.

The Chorus enters and speaks in unison: "What matters is that Anne took the initiative to *Carpe Tiempo*. We're here now. The past is over. The future can wait. How do we make this time on Earth count?"

Jane answers, "By laughing until you have to pee in your pants at least a thousand times in your life." Anne chimes in, "We should probably learn Kegels." Jane says, "Ah, heck! Just throw your underwear in the laundry and put on a fresh pair because tomorrow may be your funeral." As she utters these words she thinks of her closest high school friend, Terry, who died recently, after years of battling Crohn's disease. "Life is short," she says.

Here's a *Carpe Tiempo* tale of true love. Tim and Becky met in their mid-sixties. They were both single veterans of unhappy marriages and had pretty much given up on finding a soul mate. But when they met they fell madly in love with each other and Becky soon moved in with Tim. Shortly thereafter they invited a few friends to join them for a simple wedding outdoors in a city park. Jane recalls, "He was attracted to her fiery red hair, stiletto heels and short skirts. She loved his dry wit and his charming, gentlemanly demeanor. They were always giggling and acting like teenagers in love." Becky decorated Tim's apartment with handmade crafts and even prettied up his man cave. Tim was a two-time cancer survivor whose whole m.o. was to enjoy life and savor every moment. But after a few months of skipping through the fields of marital bliss, Tim got some bad news: a new cancer diagnosis. It was tough, but their love only deepened throughout his treatment and Tim was blessed with two years of remission.

The Chorus, wearing masks of Joy and Sorrow, speaks in unison: "Their time together helped Becky realize how lucky she was to experience the love of her life, even though their third and final year together was one of sickness and priming for death."

People tend to put off learning something new or jumping into an experience until a specific time in the future. You can't go to Europe with your spouse until the kids are older, or out of college, or until retirement. Why not go next summer? Are you letting time tick along and not jumping in? Invite him to coffee. Take that class! Buy that outfit before it goes on sale and they run out of your size! Don't put that thing off until some ambiguous time in the future. Do it now! *Carpe Tiempo!*

Like Tim and Becky, why not jump into a new relationship if your instincts are telling you there's something good here? If it doesn't work out, it doesn't work out. Many of us are afraid of judgment, or that we'll waste time by having that experience. But if it doesn't work out, you've had an experience that makes you grow. You've learned what you want and what you don't want in life. That's *Carpe Tiempo.*

Dear Reader, we admit that we are still getting a handle on this rule. So here's as good a place as any to offer a poetic phrase or two. Are we just grains of sand on the beach? Intelligent dirt? Heck, no! We are spirits cloaked in these bodies and we yearn to see the sunshine, skinny dip in the Mediterranean and party like it's 1999. *Carpe Tiempo!*

PRACTICE

To practice this rule, try seeing time as a vessel for new experiences. Think, "Time is *there,* on the early side of my next experience, as much as it is *here,* at the end of my current experience." You may procrastinate because you don't want to do a humdrum thing, like take stuff to the dump. Instead of dragging your heels and having a second cup of coffee while gazing out the window and mildly hoping it will rain, tell yourself, "I'll go have a fresh new experience and enjoy clearing a pile of junk that's been sitting around for months, if not years."

Practicing a joyful attitude as you head toward the next experience might bring a refreshing new outcome. Try applying this attitude with the same equanimity to boring actions, like finishing your income taxes, and to pleasant actions, like calling a good friend. Often, we are just getting through our daily duties. But there is meaning in those activities that seem mundane: the ritual of breakfast, lunch and dinner, clothes on, clothes off. We suggest that before you turn off the bedroom light, take an extra five minutes to review the things you are grateful for and how you've accomplished A, B and C during the day.

Carpe Tiempo means taking the time to reflect on the events in our lives and saying, "Wow, that was cool," instead of racing on to the next item of business. We so often forget to do that. Also, being early creates time. It's taken years for us to realize this. Being early gives us the time to savor time, get focused on the present, breathe before an important meeting or call Mom. Remember what the Marines always say, "If you're on time, you're already late."

A way to expand time is to learn how to slow down: participate in a yoga class, practice meditation or any other discipline that focuses the mind, like painting, practicing an instrument or lifting weights. This creates space and quiets the mind, which is often chock-full of thoughts and emotions clunking around like wet sneakers in a dryer. And, yes, Dear Reader, simply being aimless for a spell, stretching out on the couch or playing with a kitten can refresh us so that we are ever prepared to *Carpe Tiempo*.

RULE VII

PUSH ON THROUGH

RULE VII

PUSH ON THROUGH

Multiple-choice quiz; Anne and Daniel; Anne's renovation; The Second Law of Thermodynamics; Lauren's daily push; Walter's concert; Donkey Syndrome; Jane in Montana; The von Trapps; Deanna's testimony

Dear Reader, how do you spend your last night in Rome?

A. After a meal of pasta so delicious that it makes you weep, head back to the hotel and go to sleep.

B. Stroll past the illuminated ruins of the ancient city, enjoy your last cone of hazelnut gelato then go back to the hotel and go to sleep.

C. Do all of the above, but instead of going back to the hotel, go out and party with your charming new friends until continental breakfast is served at the hotel.

Can you figure this one out? If your answer was C, then you may have already mastered this rule. You may skim this chapter because you are somebody who gets the job done. You charge up that hill when the going gets tough and you say *Yes* to fun opportunities even if they are late at night. Why? Because the result will be worth it! The physical and mental fatigue you feel in that moment of resigned reasonableness — "I should turn in because I have an early flight tomorrow"— will vanish once you're settled at the bar with an impossibly curly-haired Roman eagerly fetching you a crisp gin and tonic.

If you really prefer a good night's sleep alone in your hotel during a once-in-a-lifetime trip to Rome, then, hey, no judgment. But why are you here? To study the ruins? Okay, they're pretty cool, but why did you bring that hot pink dress? Why didn't you just stay home and Marie Kondo your closet?

Perhaps this rule is not for you. You may as well sell this book for a buck twenty-five on eBay. FYI, the opposite of Push On Through is Call It a Night. We're not saying practice this rule all the time. We're saying, the practice of this rule creates opportunities to expand your horizons. Don't be so sensible. *When in*

Rome, play a little! And remember to bring the necessary precautions in your purse.

The sisters recall one night in Rome when Anne struggled with this rule. She and Jane dined on succulent ravioli and tannin-rich Montepulciano served by their attractively balding waiter named Daniel. He engagingly described the nearby farm that made the tender mozzarella and the region where the wheat was grown for the homemade pasta. When he returned at the end of the meal and poured the final drops of wine into Anne's glass, he asked discreetly if he could call her after his shift. They exchanged numbers. As the sisters went off into the balmy Roman night, the great yellow river Tiber shimmered with promise. Jane had a date lined up with a handsome shoe salesman on a Vespa. Anne went back to the hotel and wrote an encouraging text message to Daniel. His response didn't come until 2 a.m.

The next morning, over strong coffee, Jane asked coyly, "So what happened with Daniel?" Anne replied, "I decided not to meet him." Jane's mouth dropped open as she digested the news. Anne continued smugly as she nibbled her crusty breakfast roll, "He should have responded earlier to my text." Jane let it rip, "You got pissed off because it was late and on his terms. You got pouty about the small stuff and missed out on the fun you could have had with him. You cut off your nose to spite your face, you threw the baby out with the bathwater, you blew your wad!" As Anne hung her head, a shriveled wreath of laurel plopped to her feet.

The armed Minerva, definitely a Push On Through kind of gal, raised her index finger in admonition: "Had Anne practiced this rule instead of watching Italian TV in her hotel room alone, she could have had champagne and strawberries on a beach with an Italian lover!"

Some professionals have to Push On Through on a daily basis. A nurse has to get ready for her night shift after putting her kids to bed. A writer has to discipline herself to write many hours per day in order to finish her novel. A farmer has no option but to get up at dawn to feed the sheep. You get the idea. The old-timey version of Push On Through is Where There's a Will There's a Way.

There are times when just keeping up a minimum level of existence is the best you can do. You know, those times when you're feeling down and you won't even confess to your closest friend that you can barely wash your clothes or take a shower. Are you experiencing grief, burnout or depression? Did your favorite pizza pop-up move to another part of town? Our hearts go out to you. But we assure you that this, too, shall pass and this Roman Rule will have meaning for you.

Anne explains, "In Science terms, this rule is a way to combat the Second Law of Thermodynamics. When you Push On Through, you keep things from going toward maximum entropy." Jane is stumped, "Whaaat? I didn't get past eleventh-grade chemistry!" Anne explains further, "Maximum entropy means that things naturally go toward their lowest energy state. So, to put stuff back in order, you have to put in effort." Jane *pauses*. A light bulb goes off. She queries, "So the house will get dusty, and then you'll have to vacuum?" Anne replies, "Yes!" Jane continues, *"Ergo,* red roses in a vase will open up, but in time their petals will drop, so your boyfriend will have to bring you a fresh bouquet." Anne says, *"Exactement!"*

Dear Reader, remember Lauren, Anne's high school friend with the pure gray eyes? She says, "As someone who plans everything by setting goals, it was devastating when my husband of twenty-five years told me, 'I don't love you. I'm leaving.' He handed me separation papers while my father was dying in the hospital. I had never doubted that we'd be married for life. So much for love, honor and cherish for as long as you both shall live! Now that he has moved out, I've taken on his responsibilities along with all the rest of the housework. I have no choice but to Push On Through. My sons, my mom and the dog depend on me. So I have to adjust my expectations, change my plans and set new goals. Just getting through each day is how I'm pushing on through."

Minerva, mighty sage, confirmed bachelorette and daughter of Jupiter, raises her spear to Lauren, a centurion-in-training among the brave ranks of newly single moms.

We don't have all the answers. We're grabbing this lexicon and bringing it to the woman who needs to push herself to a higher level of vibration in order to experience more adventure, joy and satisfaction. This brings us back to the multiple-choice question at the beginning of this chapter. Calling it a night, putting your head on the pillow after your last day in Rome is the lowest-energy solution according to the Second Law of Thermodynamics. Therefore, this rule is a call to action, a departure from your comfort zone and a means to transcend the ordinary. Why? Because that makes life worth living. It's the stuff we put on tombstones. We're going with the gut here and feel it is our duty to share the spark of joy that we received somehow, perhaps from our father who survived the gulag with his joie de vivre intact.

Here is a recent family tale. We wanted to take our dying mother to hear our nephew's fifth-grade concert, but she couldn't be put in the car. Hospice was going to come that week and Mom would just be *à la bed* from then on, so it was going to be a wash. We almost gave up until Jane practiced this rule. With the winged feet of Mercury, she sped to Walter's elementary school to see if it was possible to push Mom there in the wheelchair. There were a few bumps and hills and the road was steep in places but it was doable. With our brother's help we got Mom in the wheelchair and literally pushed her on through to the all-purpose room of the school, then rolled her to the front row in time to see her grandson in his smart white shirt holding his huge baritone horn. He was so pleased to see his grandma. And our younger sister Carry held back tears. Mom was barely hanging in there, but she pushed on through. Everybody did.

This rule also works with laziness and procrastination. Anne is her own example. After spending two years renovating an old stone house in France, she was 90% finished when she got an offer to teach yoga for three months on a tropical island. The pay was low but the location was spectacular. Autumn was approaching and frost was on the fields. A chill was in the house and Anne would feel sorry for herself when she'd start construction work in the morning. She'd huddle over her thermos of coffee and had begun to dread her beloved power tools.

She started to suffer from *Donkey Syndrome*. What is *Donkey Syndrome*, you ask? It is a form of acute indecision, when at times we become like the proverbial donkey who can't choose between oats and hay. She swings her head from side to side trying to decide what to eat until she finally keels over from starvation.

Anne called Jane to whine about her conundrum. She so badly wanted to go teach yoga in a warm paradise, but if she put the renovation on hold, she'd lose rental income and all her momentum to finish the job when she returned. She listened attentively to her sister's wise counsel. "Put your big girl pants on!" Jane barked. "Finish the job. Next year you'll have more opportunities and you won't have to turn them down."

Anne ate some oatmeal, put on her overalls and put the rule into practice. She finished the renovation in two months, found a lovely couple to rent the place, then hopped on a flight to Southern California to visit Jane, just in time for Christmas.

You see, Dear Reader, we practice what we preach. When you are clear, and there is no more indecision, you'll find that you soar through a deadline, a first draft, a house construction. This opens the way for new experiences, which feed the soul.

Push On Through means getting to the top of the mountain. We know how Jane likes to climb trees. When she was on a summer getaway to Montana, she climbed a mountain in Glacier National Park. She could have stopped at the lookout point where most of the tourists hang out taking panoramic pictures before getting back in their cars. Instead, she joined a small group of hikers and climbed a mile farther up. Just as she reached the summit, she saw a gorgeous family of white mountain goats. And she beheld glacier lakes and snow-capped peaks as far as her eyes could see.

Are you the type of person who sits in the chalet doing a puzzle while your friends head to the top of the mountain in the ski lift? No way! Do you call it a night at 9 p.m. on New Year's Eve in LA, because the ball has dropped in Times Square? Hell, no! Would the von Trapp family not cross the Alps to escape the *Anschluss? Nein!* They pushed on through. Sometimes it gets dire out there, but centurions go the extra mile.

You can always adjust this rule to fit your personality. Lauren comments wryly, "I cannot stress enough that, yes, I am a person who would rather sit in the chalet doing a puzzle than barrel down a ski slope uncontrollably and crash into a tree." Her gray eyes sparkle: "However, I would Push On Through by snow tubing down the bunny hill, and follow that up with a Jacuzzi and spiked hot chocolate."

The sisters decide to subpoena Jane's old friend, Deanna. Remember her Jersey buddy with the Glock? She's a pure-bred Italian beauty from Fort Lee, NJ with waist-length chestnut locks and a fast right hook. Her testimony is presented below, nearly verbatim from their Zoom session. Hang on tight, Dear Reader!

"Push On Through? I know what that means. I worked three jobs so I could fly to Rome for my eighteenth birthday, and I was not impressed. I hated it. I was a platinum blonde at the time. Guys came on to me everywhere. Even at the Vatican! This guy came up to me and asked if I was American. When I said yes, he tried to kiss me. I told him, 'Get the fuck out of my face!'"

Dear Reader, we may conclude, if you go blonde and wear a double D, get ready to play ball in Rome.

Deanna continues, "I've traveled to pretty much every country where I wanted to go. I love animals so I went everywhere in Africa. All my friends, even the guys, thought I was crazy going by myself. They won't even go to a movie by themselves. They're not okay with their own thoughts. I ask them, 'When are you going to see the world? When you're old and weak? Is that when you'll go visit the gorillas, track them for eight hours into a mountain forest at high altitude with very thin air? Are you kidding me?' I went to the Peruvian Amazon with a tour group. I was 'The Bitch New Yorker.' The other gals were constantly complaining, 'There are insects and snakes in our tent.' I was like, 'Well, yeah, it's the fucking rainforest. That's why we have netting.' Birds and monkeys would come in. I loved it. One night, my tentmates started screaming about something. It was a fuzzy tarantula. I got the little guy out. Fuck, I'm not going to die from a bug!"

Anne and Jane munch on popcorn as they enjoy what comes next.

"I'm definitely more of a dude than you are, Jane," Deanna comments. "Maybe it's because I'm from a big Catholic family, I had to get used to stuff. We had to share a house with a lot of fucking people. You know how it is. We were eight kids, just like you guys, but you're not Catholic. These days, I love living alone. I like to open my fridge and find my food still there. I don't have to find my friggin' laundry on the ground. I'm definitely a tomboy. I even swam in the Amazon River. Our Peruvian guide thought I was crazy. He said, 'Do you know what's in there?' I said, 'I'm okay with it.' It was fucking hot out. I wanted to go swimming. I've survived everything: hurricanes, tornadoes, earthquakes. I was almost kidnapped in Kenya. And now I can say, I've survived a pandemic in New Jersey. The only thing I haven't been through is a tsunami. Everybody is so fearful. Fear brings on anxiety. What's gonna happen? Who cares what happens? Push On Through, dammit!"

With Deanna's final words, Jupiter throws a thunderbolt across the Hudson River, hitting a power transformer. The lights flicker. Thunder claps moments later. Deanna doesn't flinch. She glances out the window and says, "Must have hit Hoboken."

PRACTICE

To practice this rule, you must resist the temptation to wimp out. You are exhausted from a day of sightseeing and you've relished a delicious pasta followed by luscious tiramisu and icy, tart *limoncello,* brought by a sexy, slightly balding waiter. The hotel pillows will be calling you, but you must fight the immediate gratification of a soft bed in exchange for an adventure or perhaps a romantic romp accompanied by moonlight, fresh peaches and a strapping Roman lover.

We can practice this rule in any number of life situations. And guess what, you workaholics? This may be the hardest rule for you in many ways because Push On Through doesn't just mean putting in overtime, winning the contract or pleasing the boss. It also means you have to get out of the office early to see your child's performance in *Charlotte's Web*, join the tag football team at work to be social or just get home at a reasonable time to relax on the couch with your partner and uncork the pinot noir. Yes, many of us will have to Push On Through in order to get more rest. If, on the other hand, you're a procrastinator who suffers from *Donkey Syndrome*, just choose the oats every time. They're gluten free.

What can hinder you from succeeding with this rule? Basically, stagnation and inaction. One big factor is doubt. Doubt will hold you back more than almost any other thing. Practice making decisions: make them fast, make them slow. Just make them, you'll get better at it. And consider getting a life coach to build your confidence.

Another big factor is negative thinking. There are myriad ways to shift into a more positive mindset. Learn meditation. Read uplifting literature. Listen to joyful music. Spend more time with people who inspire you. Join a charity, a bowling league, a spiritual group. Watch more comedies, less news, and laugh!

Dear Reader, beware of the company you keep. You may have to say goodbye to negative "friends" who try to sink your ship. True friends help each other out. Yet, there may still be times when you have to talk yourself off a ledge. So it's helpful to have a strategy to lift yourself up and be your own cheerleader. Jane asks, "When you've been moping, do you sometimes give yourself a little swat and say, 'At least I'm not in the *gulag'?"* Anne answers, "Yes, that helps."

In the event that you are having trouble applying this rule ... go to Rome. Treat it like a business trip. This is important, people! Just buy the plane ticket. Call in sick and go for a long weekend. Practice Push On Through. As Thoreau says, you don't want to find out when it comes time to die that you have never lived. The key here is to balance work, rest *and* play.

$$\Delta S \equiv \frac{\Delta Q}{T}$$

BONUS RULE

LET
IT
GO

BONUS RULE

LET IT GO

Lynn's yoga class; Lauren's song; Kelly and Charlie; Cheryl and Jeremy; Amy and TJ; Jane's divorce; Anne's divorce; The takeaway

Congratulations, Dear Reader, you now know *The Seven Roman Rules* and you are on your way to becoming a centurion. We commend you for your determination and award you with this final bonus rule. It is a last-ditch, throw-the-switch, ejector-seat button to use when a relationship is at its end.

There comes a time when we recognize that the end has come. A time to do what Lynn, our wise yoga teacher, said at our New Year's Day class: "Stop holding on to a picture of something that is no longer reality, even if it seems too scary to let go." The *Titanic* was wrecked on an iceberg and the end had clearly come. It was time to jump ship. Even the great civilization of Rome fell. But how do you know the end has come in your relationship? Sometimes it's not that obvious.

Wait, hold everything! Hold that question while we ask you the following: have you achieved balance in your life or are you still relying on your mate to satisfy your needs? Did you attempt to spice things up or are you just bored? In simple terms, did you sincerely implement each of the Roman Rules? Or did you skip one, perhaps? Maybe you're still not convinced that Age Is Irrelevant. Or somewhere in the back of your mind you don't Trust the Heat. *Pause.* Breathe. Go through the list. Check each rule twice. Get a trusted friend to give you the *straight dope.*

Are you with us? A Roman centurion puts in the effort, brings her best self to the office, to friendships and to her love relationships. And when they don't work out, she doesn't cast blame or get spiteful. If you have applied all seven rules, we commend you, Budding Centurion. You are welcome to invoke the bonus rule. Shrug your shoulders. Take a deep breath. Throw your arms up to the sky and say it loud and clear: "I Let It Go!"

Some of us are familiar with the Law of Detachment. This law says that by letting go, you make a decision to release your attachment to the outcome. Many sages have been thus inspired by this law in the *Bhagavad*

Gita, India's #1 best seller for the last three thousand years. Anne says thoughtfully, "This is so profound, I wonder *how* we can even advise our readers to Let It Go?" Jane ponders this for a moment, then says, "Get a pet. That's what my friend Anthony did. He was tired of his relationships not working out, so he got a dog."

If the job is intolerable, quit. You weren't born with it and you won't die with it. If a so-called "friend" keeps rescheduling lunch, stop the Hollywood shuffle and drop the friend. After a decade of trying to win over your in-laws, invoke this rule. Who knows, maybe when they're old and gray, you'll become the best of friends.

Jane was asked to give the straight dope on her friend's relationship. Kelly, a soft-spoken biologist, told her that she was at the brink of a breakup. Her boyfriend, Charlie, was quite a bit younger than she. Jane recalled that in the beginning they were madly in love and Kelly invited him to move in. She helped him launch a landscape business, but once it began to turn a profit the focus was no longer on each other.

Kelly was sanguine, at first. She started going to yoga and fostering a cat. But she confessed, "We haven't gone out on a date in months. The business is going great, but he doesn't offer to help pay for rent or utilities." Jane scratched her head and asked, "Do you at least have good sex?" Kelly sighed, "Well, if he makes it home before I fall asleep." Jane's eyeballs rolled. Kelly said, quietly, "I guess I could tell it was coming to an end when he asked me to pay for the handyman jobs he does around the house." Jane's forehead clunked audibly onto the table as she queried, "He doesn't charge you a cuddling fee?"

Jane sighed and gave Kelly the straight dope. "You wanted a life partner so you've been putting up with his late nights and no dates. And Charlie stopped showing you the books when his business took off." Kelly winced a little, then said, "Since we were in love, I didn't bring it up. And now it seems somehow too late." Jane raised one eyebrow: "You should have communicated about that. That's Follow Through, rule number two."

Sibyl, the ancient Roman fortune teller, cackled and interjected, "You can't squeeze blood from a turnip."

Jane pondered this truth for a moment and told Kelly, "You trusted the Heat. You grew your mojo. Age was clearly irrelevant—he was ten years younger. You told him you needed help with rent and getaway time with him, but he thought he could get away with just doing chores. Sorry. This doesn't cut it in Rome or in your home."

Sibyl intoned, "You gave it a good Roman try. You may now invoke the bonus rule!"

An owl shrieked.

Kelly raised her arms to the crescent moon and exclaimed, "I Let It Go!"

The bonus rule is not about giving up. It is about surrendering to a higher intention beyond your own hurts and desires. It is about letting yourself and the whole universe know that you are ready to close one door and open a new one.

Lauren, our gray-eyed computer-scientist and budding centurion, gives this keen advice: "If you're feeling blue, just play the hit song *Let It Go* from *Frozen* over and over again. Sing it. Sing it away!"

Sometimes you don't need to Let It Go. Several years ago, Anne counseled her friend Cheryl, a beautiful redhead, about her marriage with Jeremy. They were both talented actors and musicians who loved each other, but they were at the brink of divorce. Jeremy was jealous that Cheryl's acting career took her to Greece and other exotic locations. He would phone her every day and mistrusted her when he couldn't get ahold of her. Cheryl bristled, "It's stifling and exhausting." Anne asked, "Do you love him?" Cheryl nodded, with tears in her eyes. Anne continued, "If you do, you need to reassure him and tell him you need his trust. You both must accept that there will be Collaborative Heat with fellow artists from time to time. It doesn't mean either of you will act on it."

Cheryl told Jeremy the straight dope and he flexed because his love ran deep. They communicated about his insecurities and they started rebuilding trust. There was still Heat in the relationship. Now they are very happy and there's a baby on the way. Cheryl was smart. One can work on jealousy with direct communication and motivation, like she did. There was no reason to Let It Go. She just had to speak up, loud and clear.

Amy, a twentysomething florist, confided in Jane about her breakup a year before with her college boyfriend, TJ, a wealthy young man with doting parents. TJ was tall, dark and sexy. Perfect hair, perfect smile. A straight-A student who rarely needed to study, and he excelled at varsity sports. He drove a fancy car that talked. "Things came easy to him and I guess I was one of those easy things," Amy said with candor. "I'm a simple person, but I always wanted a special gift from TJ: Coco Chanel parfum. Christmas passed, he didn't give it to me, my birthday passed, he didn't give it to me. Another year, another birthday, still no parfum. On our last Christmas, he gave me Coco Chanel, but it was eau de toilette. It didn't smell as good. I was thinking, 'You have money, you're driving a Porsche, it should be parfum.'" Jane nodded and asked, "Was it too little too late?" Amy confessed, "Oh, you know, it wasn't really about the gift. I learned that he didn't value family the way I did. On Thanksgiving, he just wanted to hang out with friends and do football-pool gambling at a bar. And, yeah, his mom still did his laundry. I needed someone more independent."

Rather than compromise the things she valued in her life, Amy ended the relationship with TJ, the young man who had it all, except her heart. She Let It Go. And within a month she started seeing Vince, a single dad from a big, loving family. She smiled and held up her left hand so Jane's eyes could feast on a sparkling rock, set in white gold.

These testimonials may remind you of your own Aha! moments. Relationships are complicated, communication is never perfect. But when you have made the effort and taken action, when you have shown maturity and tolerance, but to no avail, you can invoke the bonus rule.

Anne and Jane *pause*. "Okay, Anne, it's time to get real with our readers about the end of our marriages," Jane declares. Anne agrees, "No time like the end of the book, right?"

"Okay, I'll start," Jane mutters. "I got tired of playing wife to a husband with a political career. We grew apart, pursuing our individual goals." Anne waits. Then says, "Well, *that* sure does sum it up in a nutshell. Jane, let's give our readers the straight dope here. Jane thinks a moment, then dives in:

"We were building our careers and we were classic workaholics. I waited tables and Saul worked twelve-hour days at the U.S. Mission to the United Nations. Then we'd eat out or order in. Lots of pasta and bagels." Anne says, "Yeah, I remember your fridge. There was no food in there. It was a white, empty cube. In yoga, good, fresh food is vital for your well-being." Jane remarks, "Yes, I have learned a lot since then! Ours was the typical New York lifestyle. I was acting, singing, producing theatre and wearing a lot of black. There was always noise … from the city outside and inside the apartment, too. The TV was constantly on with political news. It started to drive me nuts." Anne chimes in, "I know you need your quiet time, after growing up in *our* house."

Jane resumes, "I didn't communicate about that with him, or about needing more intimate time together. We didn't *do* date nights. Our getaway time was mainly spent visiting his family. I did enjoy a few cruises with Saul and his dad. But I found myself growing resentful." Jane lowers her voice. "The deeper issue was, we didn't have Heat. You think it's normal until you finally know better. My best friend told me, 'Jane, you just need getaway time for yourself.' Well, I never claimed that time for myself, or with him. But I needed it so much. After our breakup, I remember going out to Jones Beach and enjoying being at the ocean and wishing I had done that during our marriage."

Anne offers, "You didn't know *The Seven Roman Rules* back then." Jane agrees, "I didn't have a clue about trusting the Heat or growing my mojo. I just didn't have the balls to say all the things I wanted. Then Dad died and I had such deep sadness I closed myself off to Saul. We had never learned to communicate those deeper feelings." Anne asks, "Isn't that when you started thinking about having a baby?" Jane says, "Yes, but that just put another kibosh on intimacy."

Anne notices her sister lost in thought. "Jane, everybody thought you were the perfect couple. What made you finally Let It Go with Saul?" Jane answers, her voice brittle, "He wanted to move to New Jersey for his career. I wanted to be in the West Village, pursuing theatre! There was no way I was going to move to the suburbs." Anne asks, "Did you think he would have said no if you had asked him?" Jane answers, "I guess I thought it was too late. There was a line in the sand."

Anne sets a laurel wreath on her sister's blonde hair.

Anne says, "I guess it's my turn." She begins her tale: "I had been nerding out in libraries for years, getting degrees. Then, at my renewable energy training in Corsica, I met Vincent and my biological clock went off. I wanted to nest with him. He brought me to the middle of nowhere to live, near a sheep farm in southwest France. I embraced that but it was so far from my Paris home, I had to subscribe to *Paris Match,* a gossip magazine, to feel connected to my former city life. Vincent was French, with Portuguese parents. His father had been a shepherd, like his grandmother. Communication was challenging at times. I remember a friend of ours once said we were the most different people he had ever met in a couple. He remarked, 'That only works if things are good in the bedroom *or* if you have children. You have no kids, so I guess the sex is good.' Vincent and I did not disagree with him. There was so much Heat. Right up until the end we'd hold hands when we'd fall asleep."

Jane summarizes, "Anne, you practiced a few of the rules, pre-Rome. You married a younger man, so age was irrelevant. You started your wind-energy business together, so you pushed on through. You seemed to *Carpe Tiempo* by learning outdoor sports with him like rock climbing. And you trusted the Heat. I thought Vincent was a good match for you. But I noticed you were beginning to lose your mojo during your marriage. You gained fifteen pounds and you stopped wearing sexy clothes. What went wrong?"

Anne dives in, "Our adventures stopped when our business took over. Our offices were in our house. We were together 24-7. Forget date nights. We didn't even go to the one restaurant in our ancient little village! If we had our own separate hobbies, friends or family nearby we could have had a more balanced life." Jane comments, "That's all shoulda, woulda, coulda." She asks, "Didn't you have animals, like that cool donkey?" Anne shakes her head, "You mean Pompon? He was the neighbor's. He had a nasty temper." "Who, Vincent?" Jane asks. "Yeah, him, too," Anne admits, quietly, "At times, he'd cut me down in front of friends and colleagues." She pauses, then says, "I remember the constant feeling that I was running out of time. I wanted to start a family and stop climate change all at once. But he wanted to wait on having children. We waited a bit too long."

Jane takes her laurel wreath and places it upon her sister's lowered head.

The sisters hold masks of sorrow in front of their faces.

Jane: My husband had a jealous streak and didn't love it if I dressed up and put on perfume. Of course, there were exceptions, like Valentine's Day or our anniversary.

Anne: I felt I had to take care of my partner's needs, but I didn't know how to ask him to take care of mine.

Jane: I sure thought my marriage was going to be for life. I thought we'd be rocking on the porch laughing together as old people. The laughter would always be there.

Anne: We moved into our new house after the miscarriage. It felt like the walls were closing in on me. I knew he would want a family, eventually, but it would be too late for me. I asked for the separation.

Chorus: Anne and Jane grew up at the tail end of an era where black-and-white TV shows still championed traditional female roles. Yet their mother's mantra was: "Never marry. Don't have kids. Make your own money." They grew up thinking you couldn't have a happy marriage and a successful career. But maybe the guys would have met them in the middle?

The sisters lower their masks.

Jane says, "It took a lot of courage to leave our relationships without knowing what we would lose: comforts, companionship and, what's that word …

security?" Anne chuckles, "Someone to bring in the wood and start the fire. Someone to make you go rock climbing over a rugged shore. Someone to cook meat for." Jane smiles. "I've been pretty lucky with my men. They've all been kind and decent." Anne nods in agreement and adds, "I was afraid of settling down because I thought I'd be controlled. But I was the one holding the remote the whole time."

Jane remarks, "Anne, we learned resourcefulness and independence at an early age from our older siblings and parents." Anne agrees, "Mom and Dad taught us to value experience more than material gain. We backpacked across Europe when you were sixteen and our brother was fourteen." Jane recollects fondly, "And you were our leader at eighteen! We loved it. Especially Rome. Our centurion spirit was forged there."

So, what's the takeaway, Dear Reader? Life is short! Whether it's a rocky relationship that zaps your strength, a boss you just can't please or a needy friend you can no longer uplift, you've given it your best. Now what? First you practice the Roman seven. Then you try everything else: therapy, bungee jumping, a pet. But when nothing helps, how do you get off the crazy train?

The answer comes like a whisper from the ruins of ancient Rome on a moonlit night: Let It Go.

> Jane: I think this is a wrap.
> Anne: Hit save!
> Jane: Over ten years in the making.
> Anne: Centurions Follow Through.
> Jane: Chianti?
> Anne: Let's go celebrate.

The clouds part and show the Roman goddesses and gods raising their chalices in a toast. The Chorus waves goodbye as the sisters walk toward the setting sun.

ABOUT THE AUTHORS

Jane is an actress and award-winning producer. She studied and performed on the stage in the DC area after completing her B.A. in International Communications at The George Washington University. Her theatrical ambitions brought her to New York where she studied and performed Off Off Broadway and became Artistic Director of P.A.C.T. (Playwrights/Actors Contemporary Theatre). She co-founded SkyTown Entertainment, a full-service bi-coastal video production company that specializes in self-tape auditions for actors. She currently lives in Los Angeles where she continues to act, produce, write, sing and play her guitar.

Anne entered the world as an actress and storyteller. Her curiosity led her to train as a physicist at national laboratories in the USA and in France. While obtaining her Doctorate in Paris, she explored the great cities of Europe as an adjunct science professor, English teacher, literary and scientific editor, and roadie with a Czech rock band. Concern for the planet's future led her to create a renewable energy company in southwest France with her then partner. Yoga took her further afield to India, where she worked with non-profit organizations and trained in Ayurveda. Anne now lives in the Washington, DC area.

Visit us at www.thesevenromanrules.com to sign up for our newsletter and receive updates about our journey with the book!

Printed in Great Britain
by Amazon